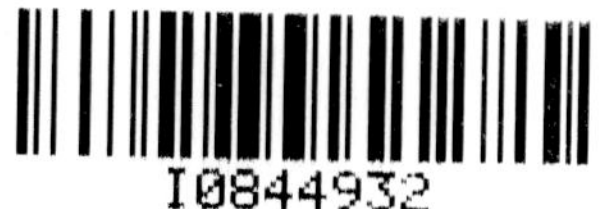

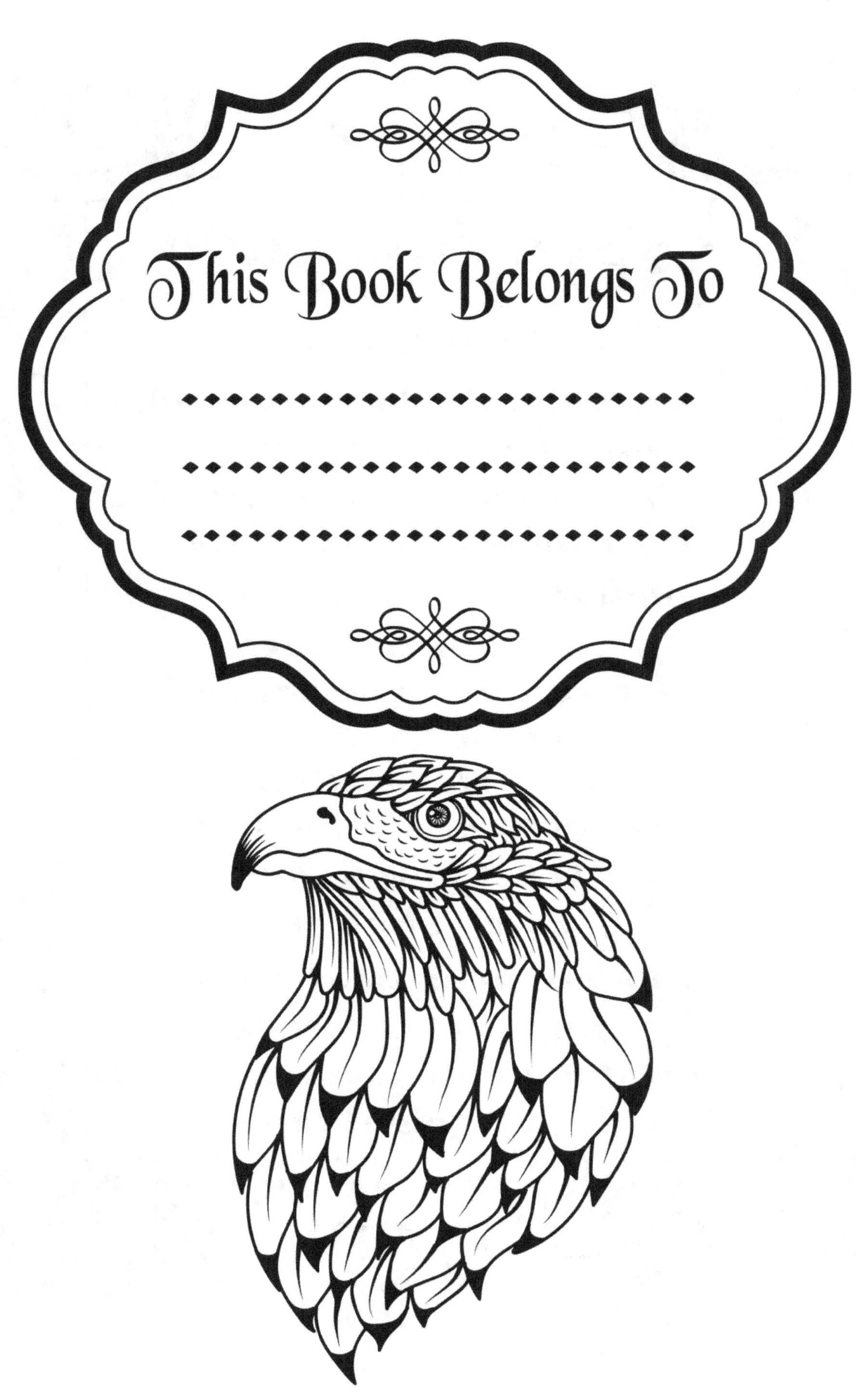

This Book Belongs To

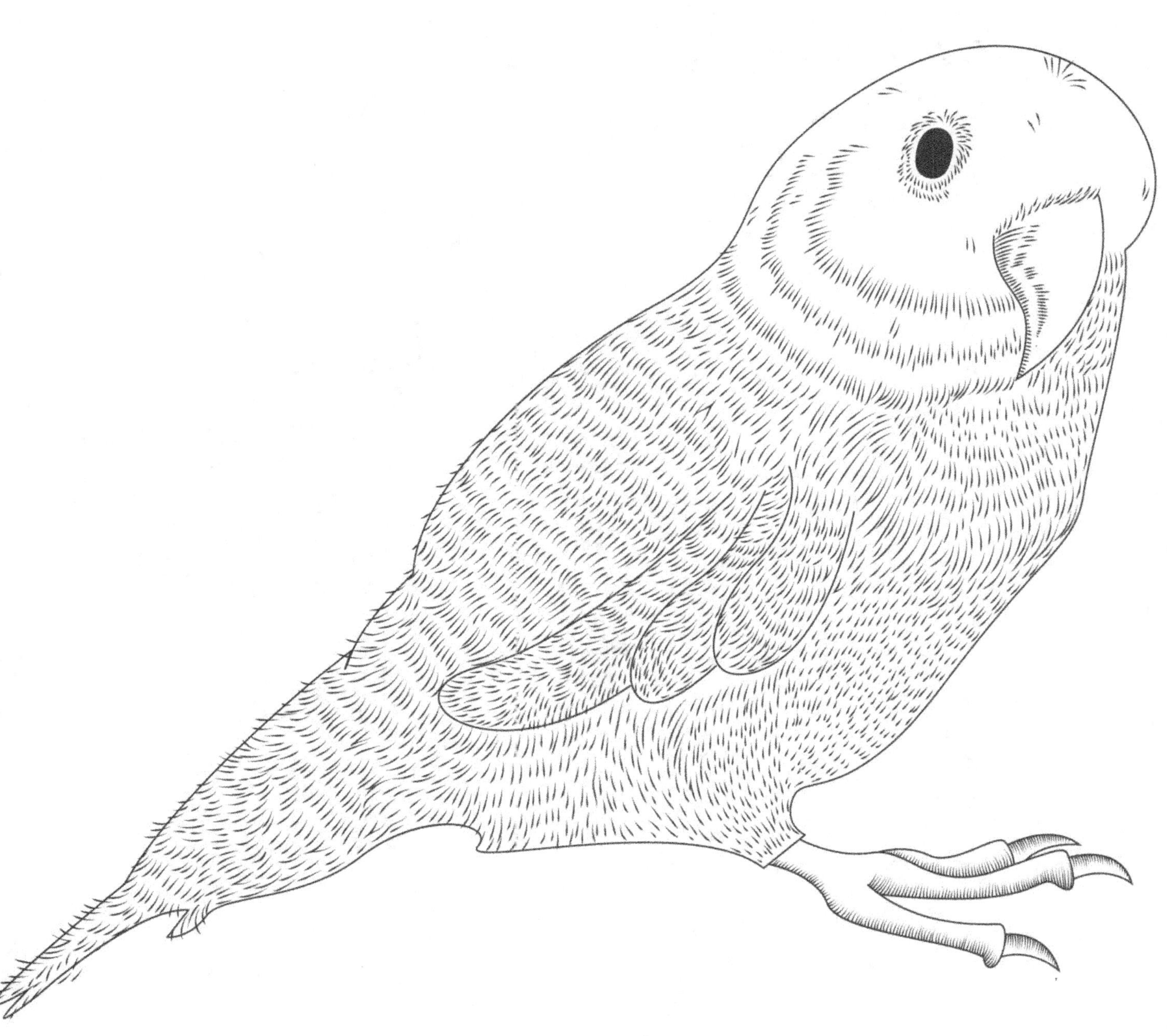

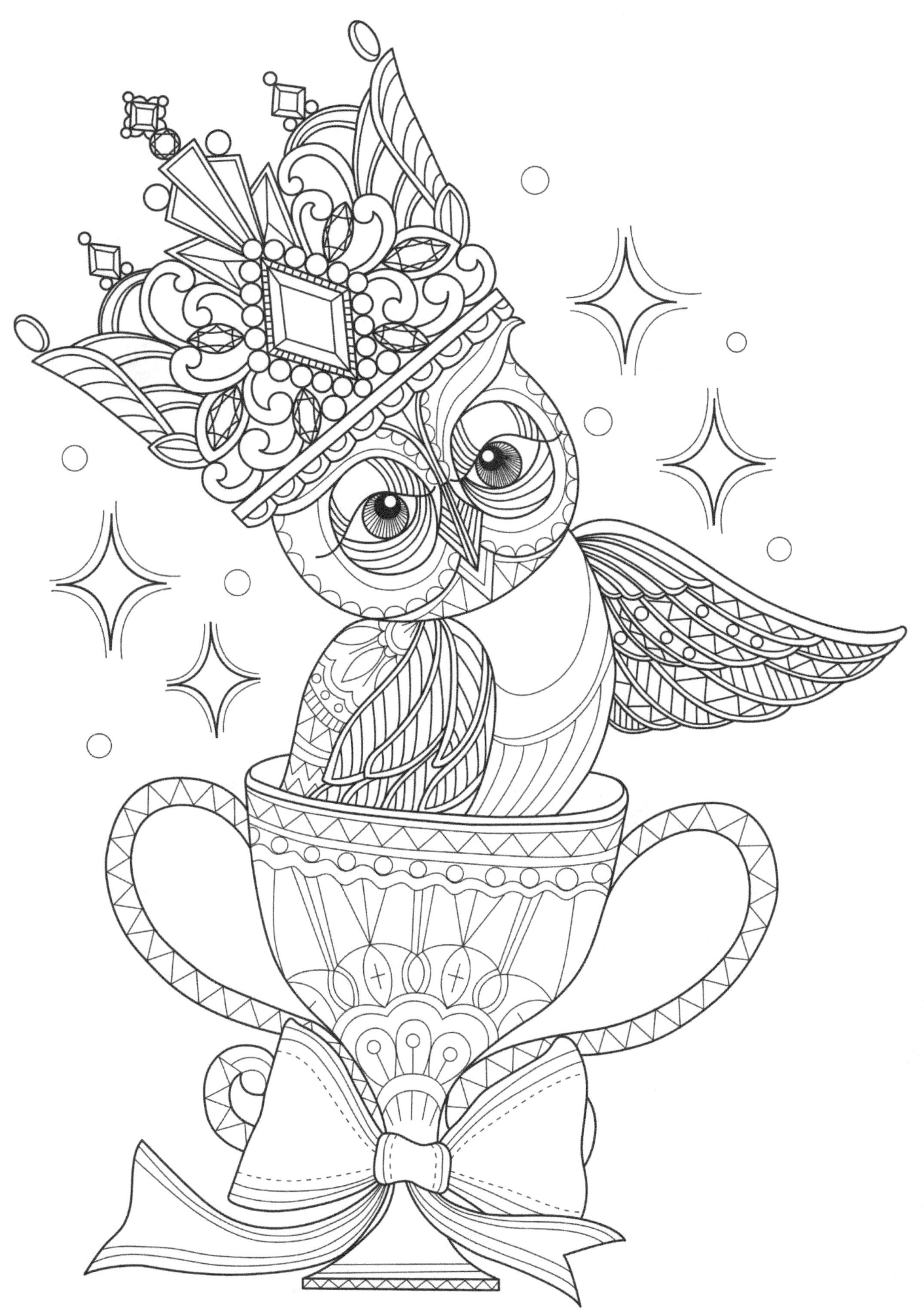

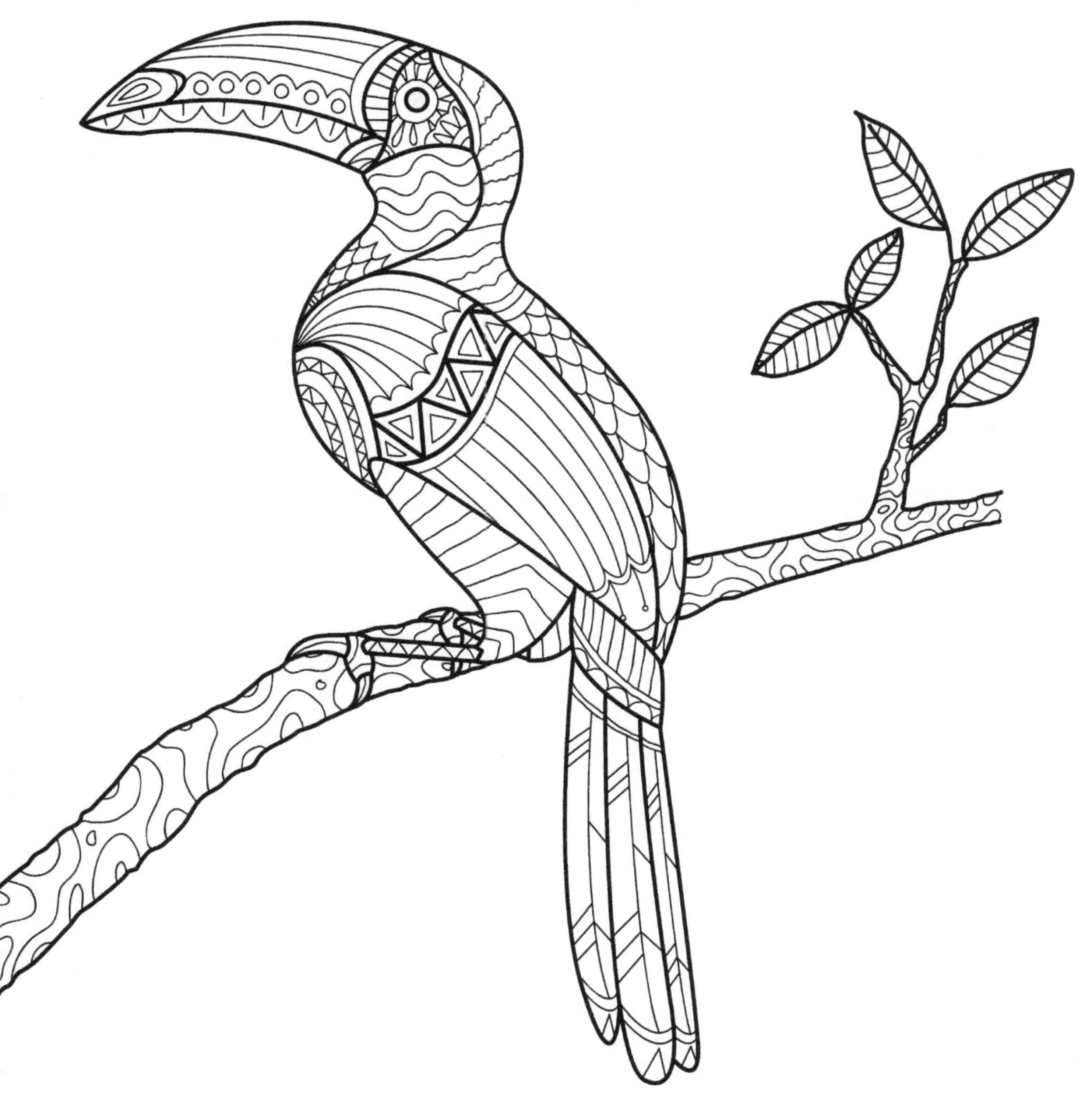

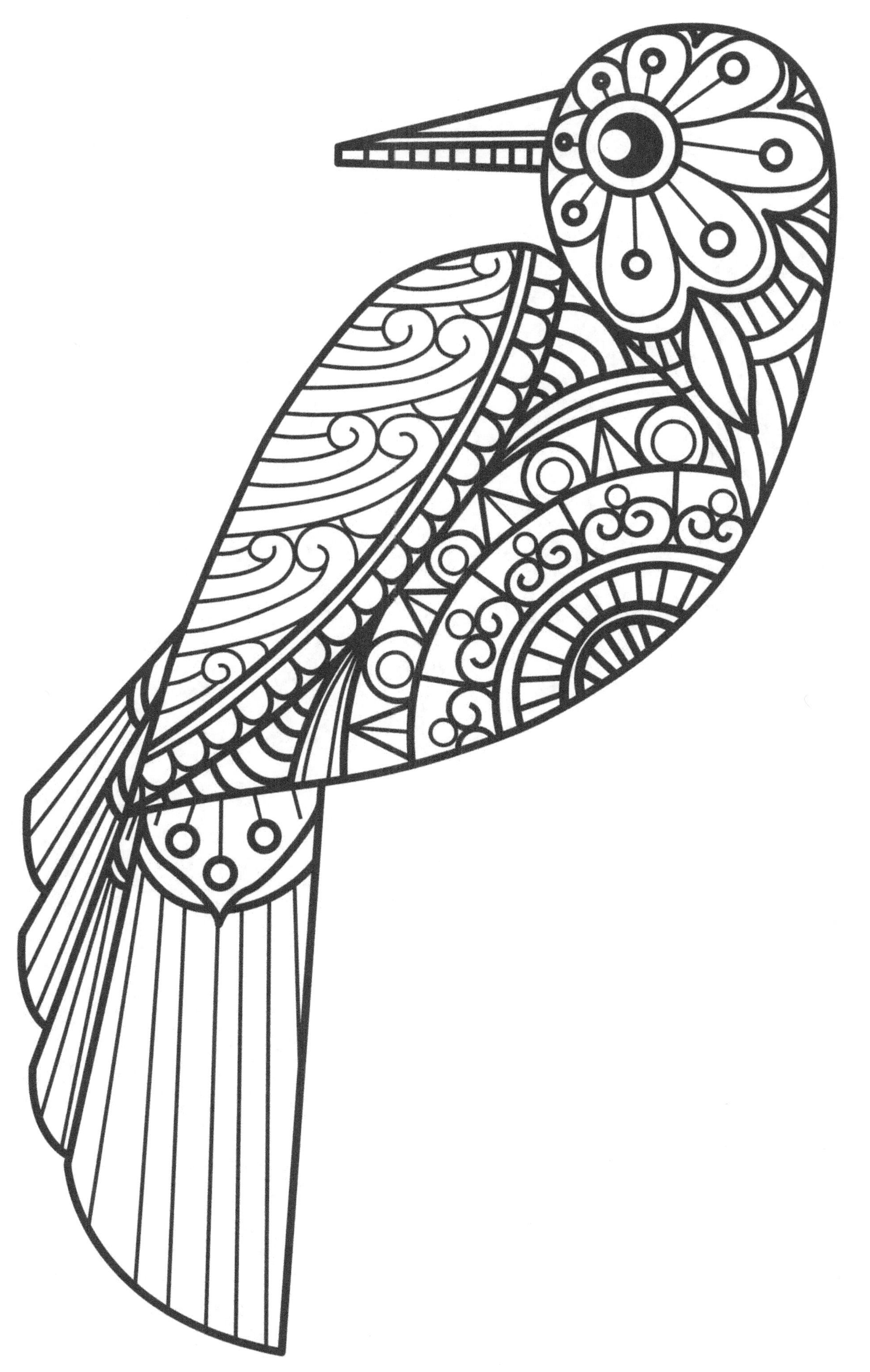

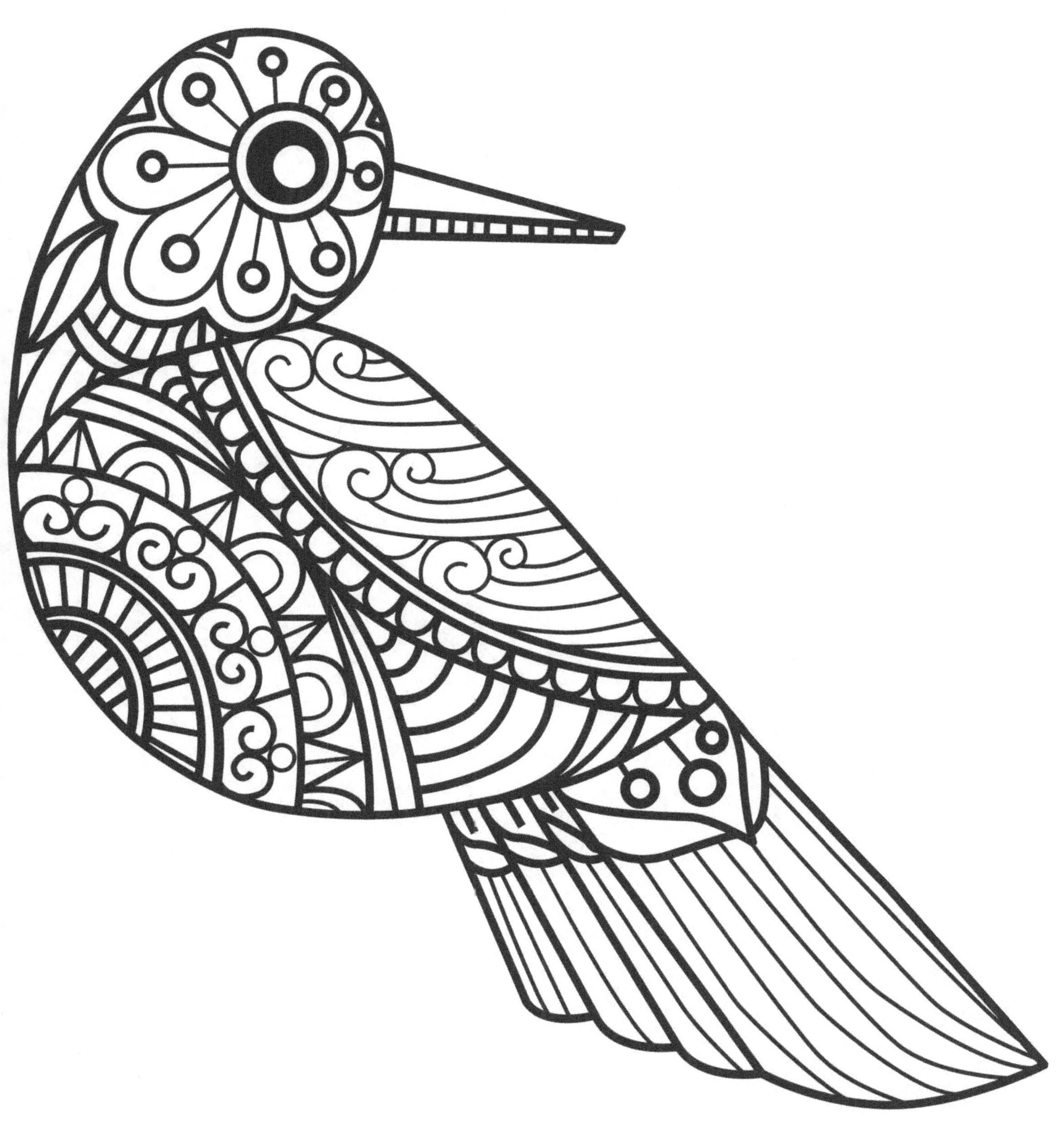

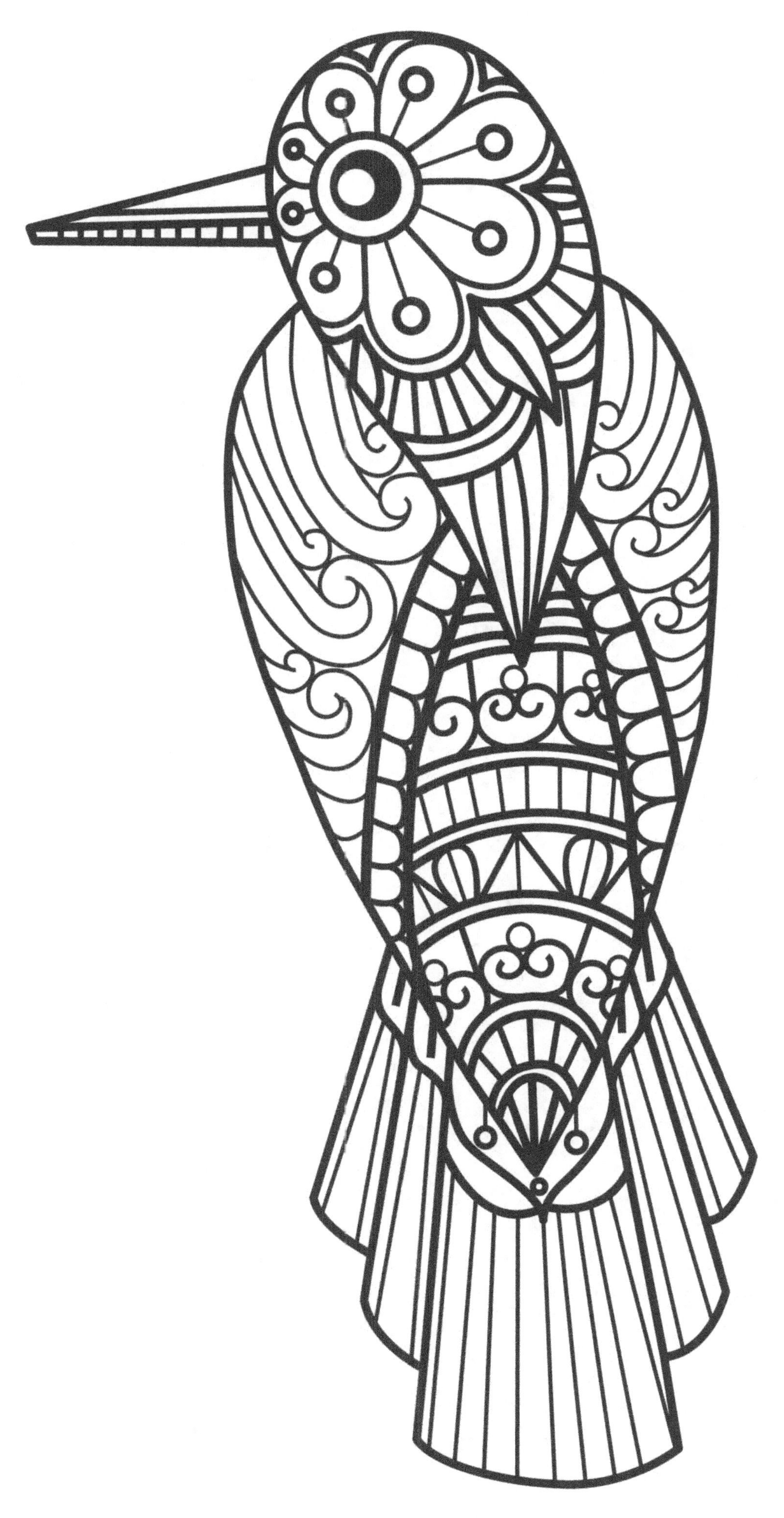

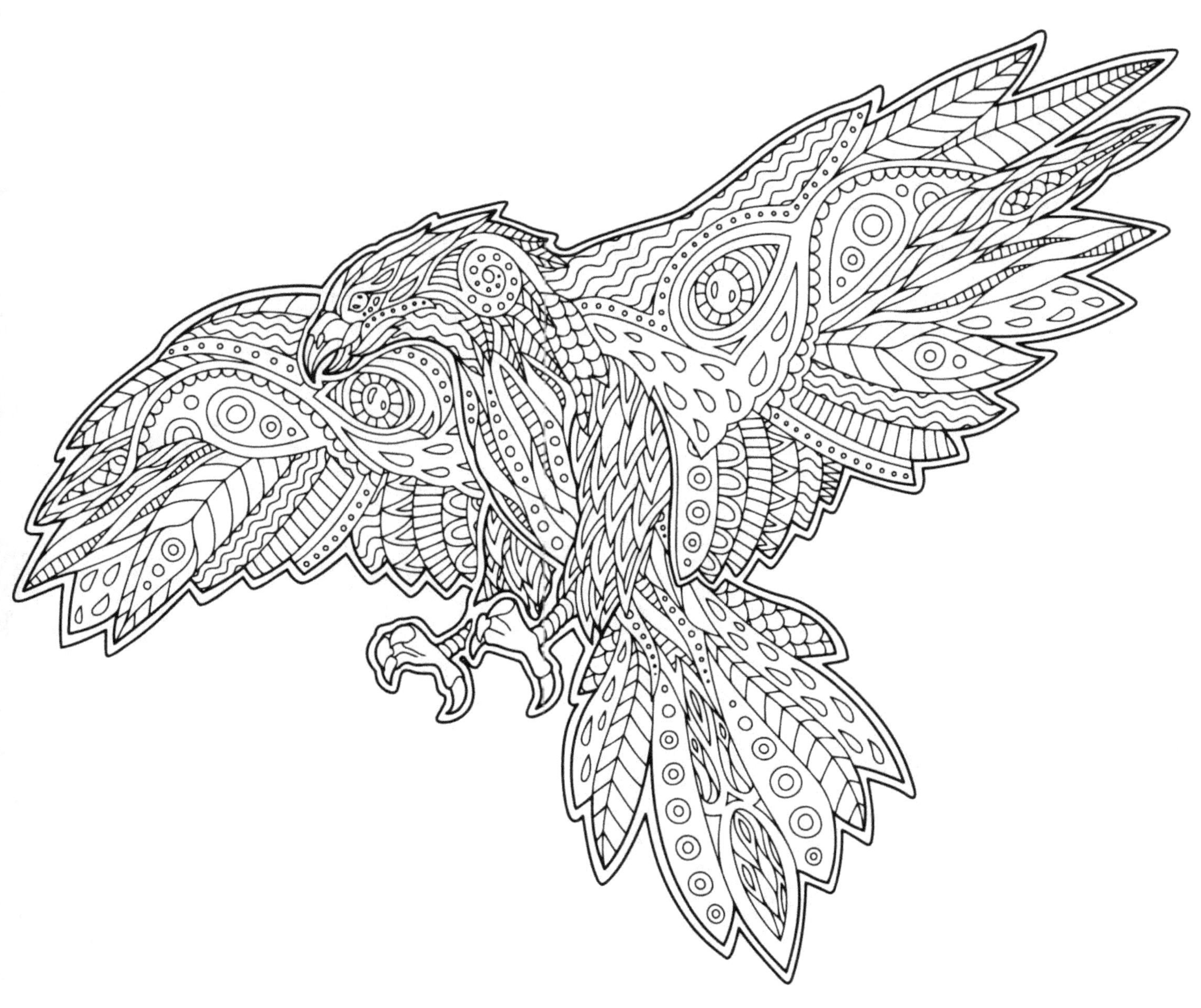

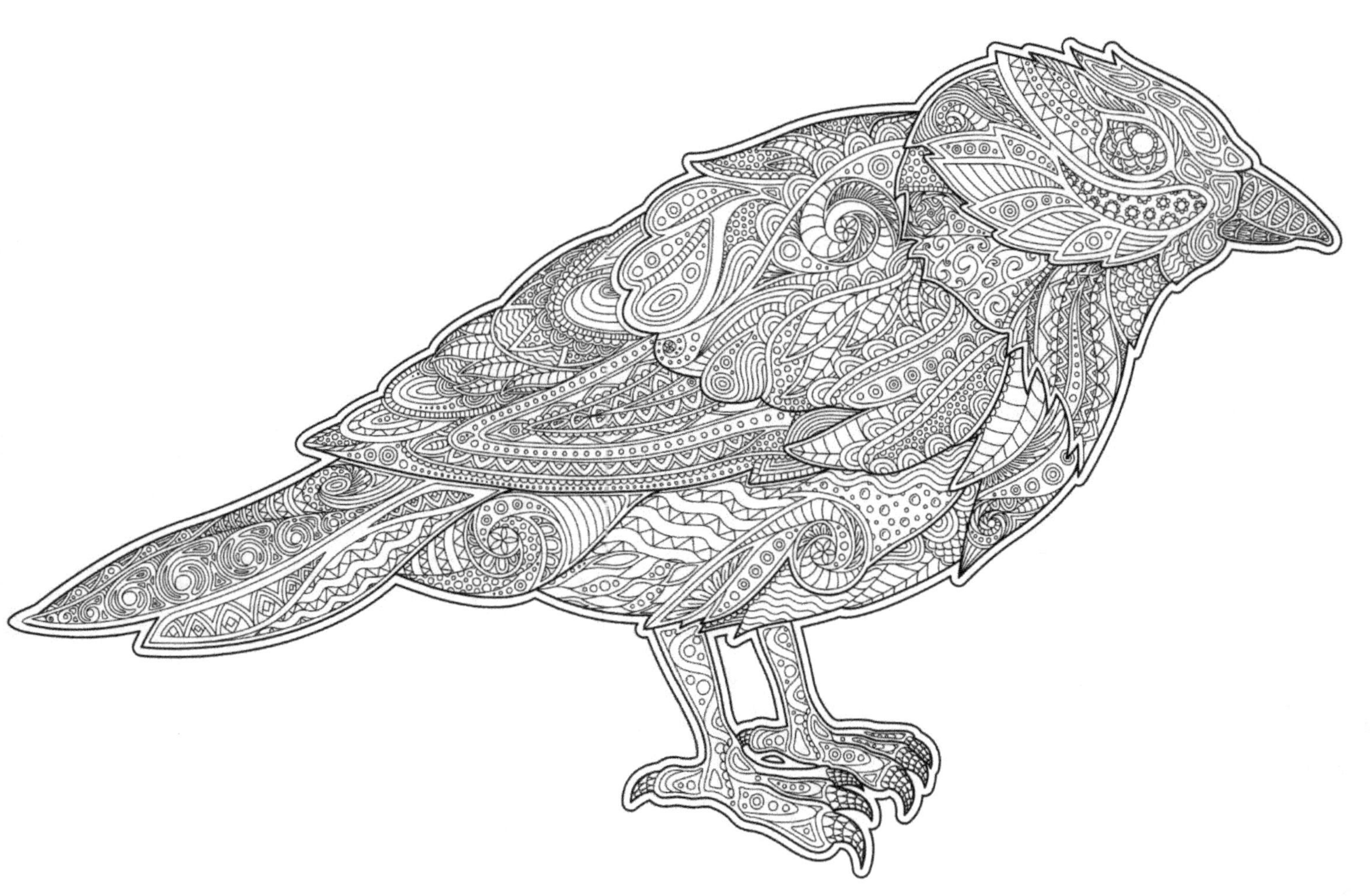

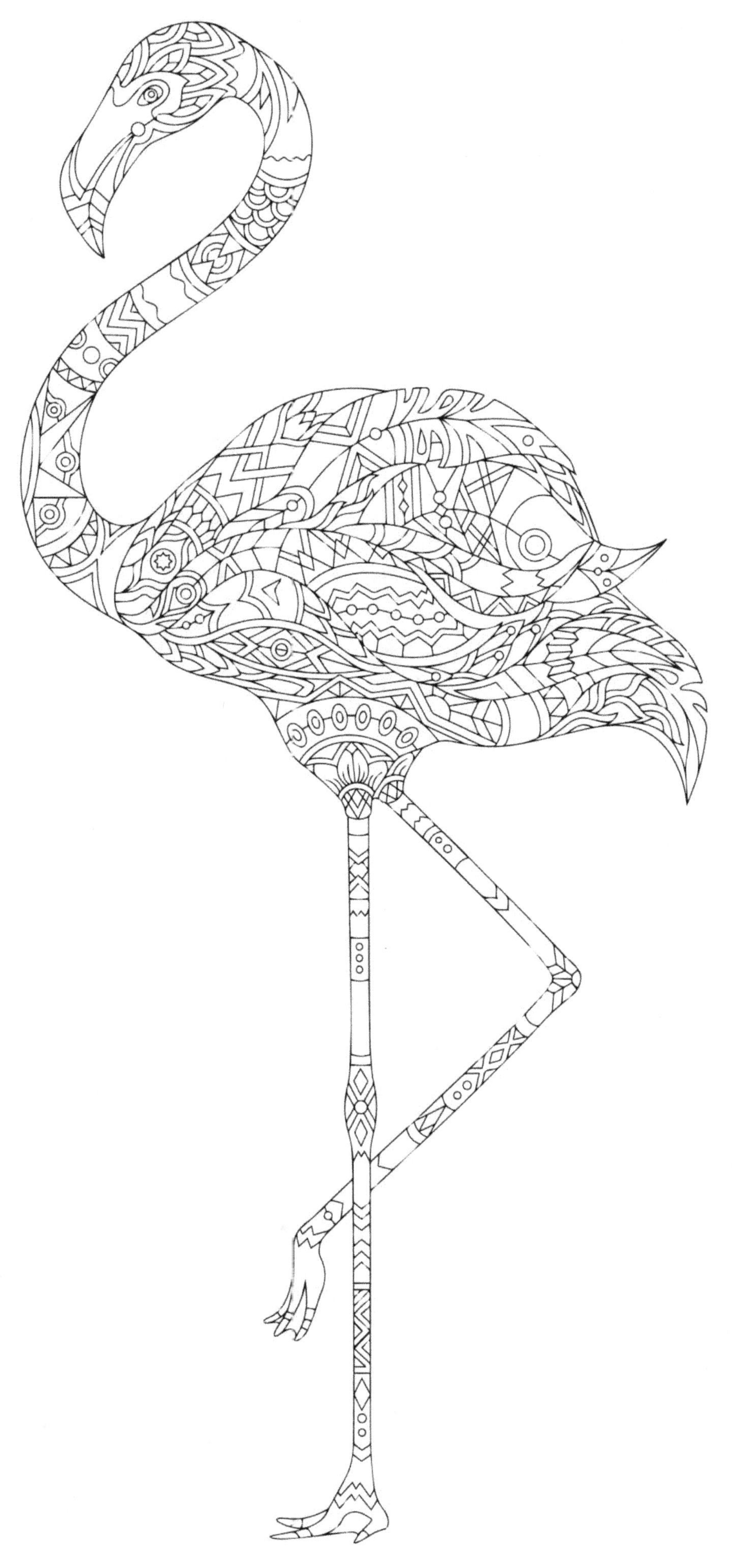

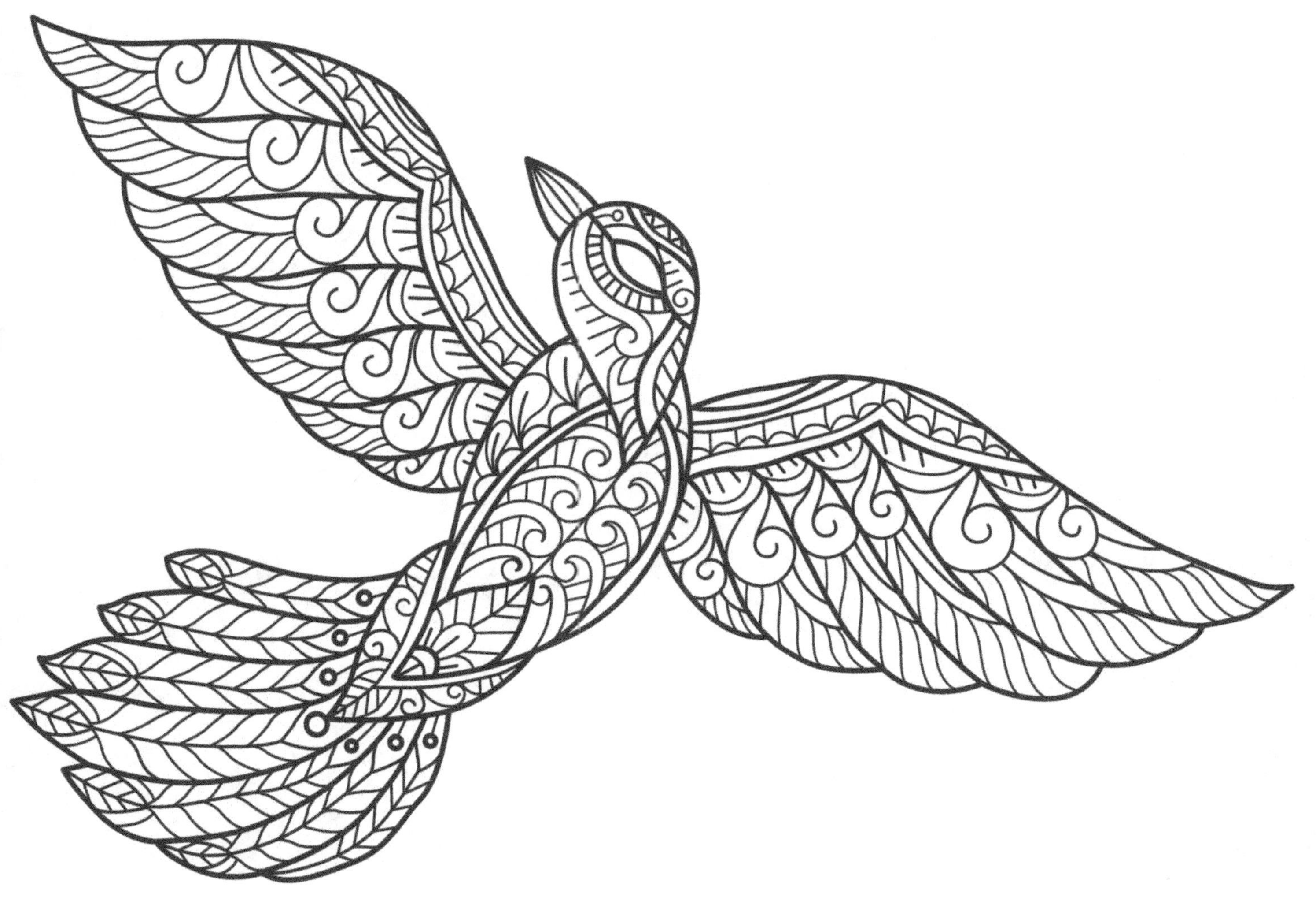

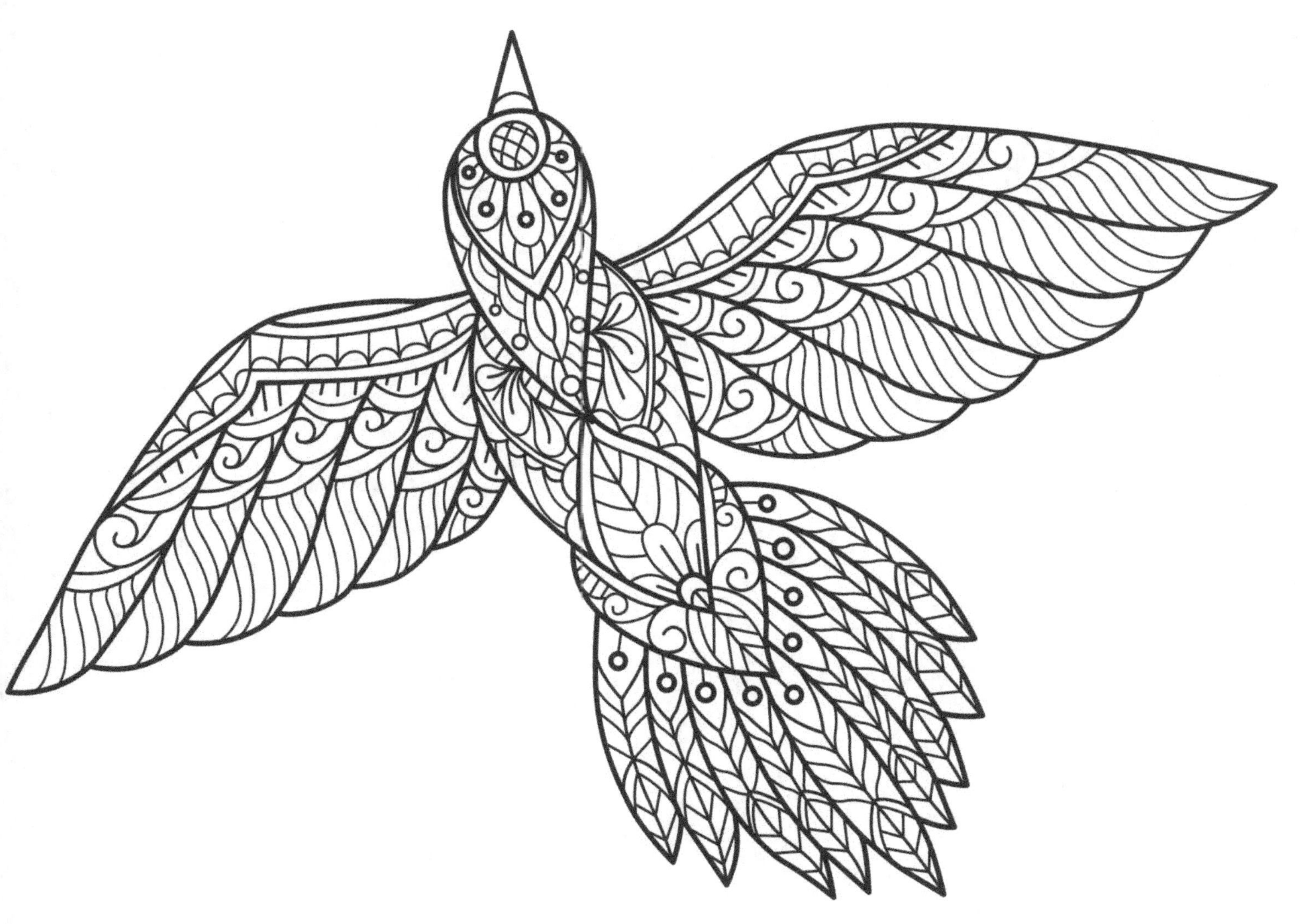

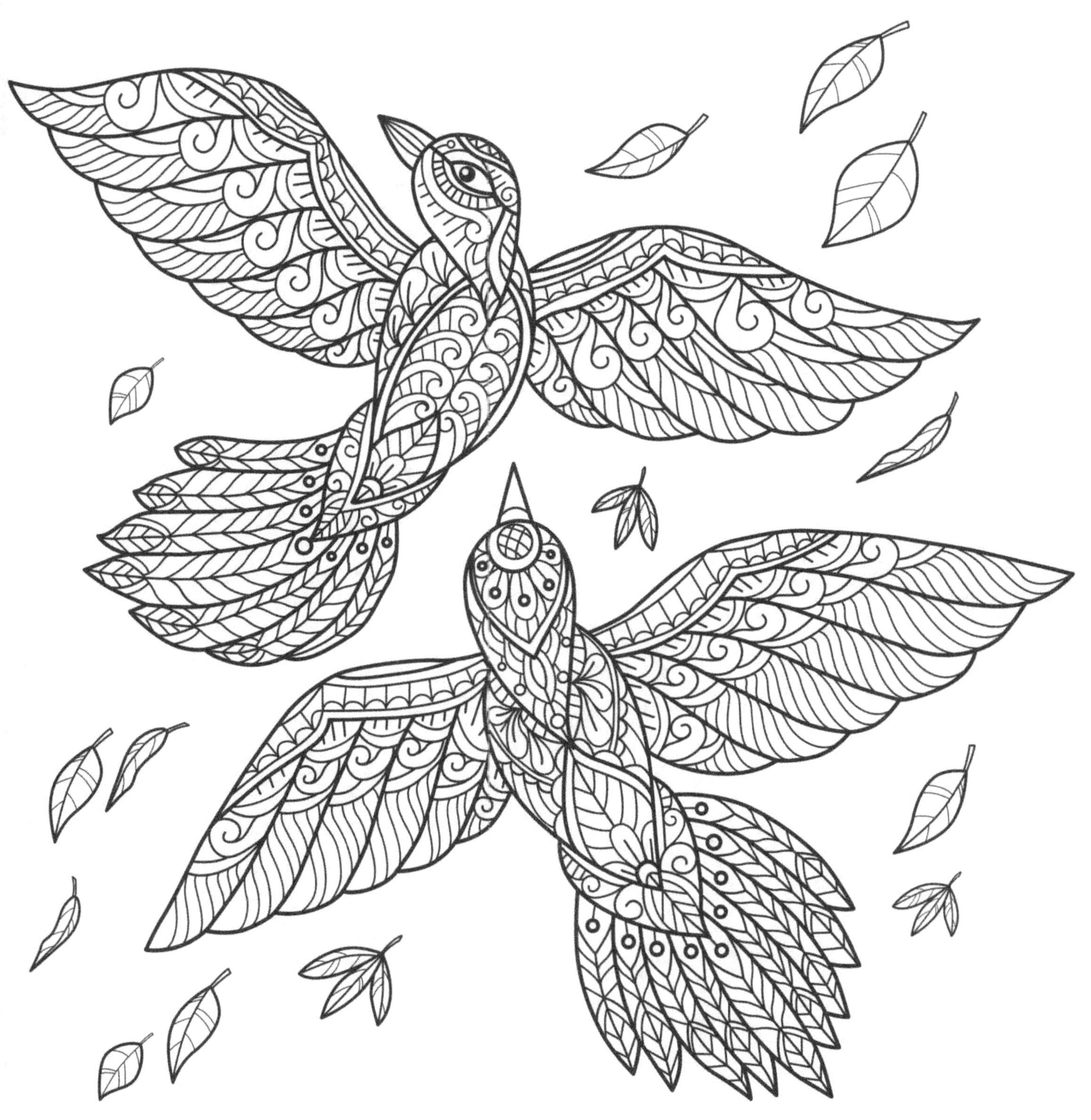

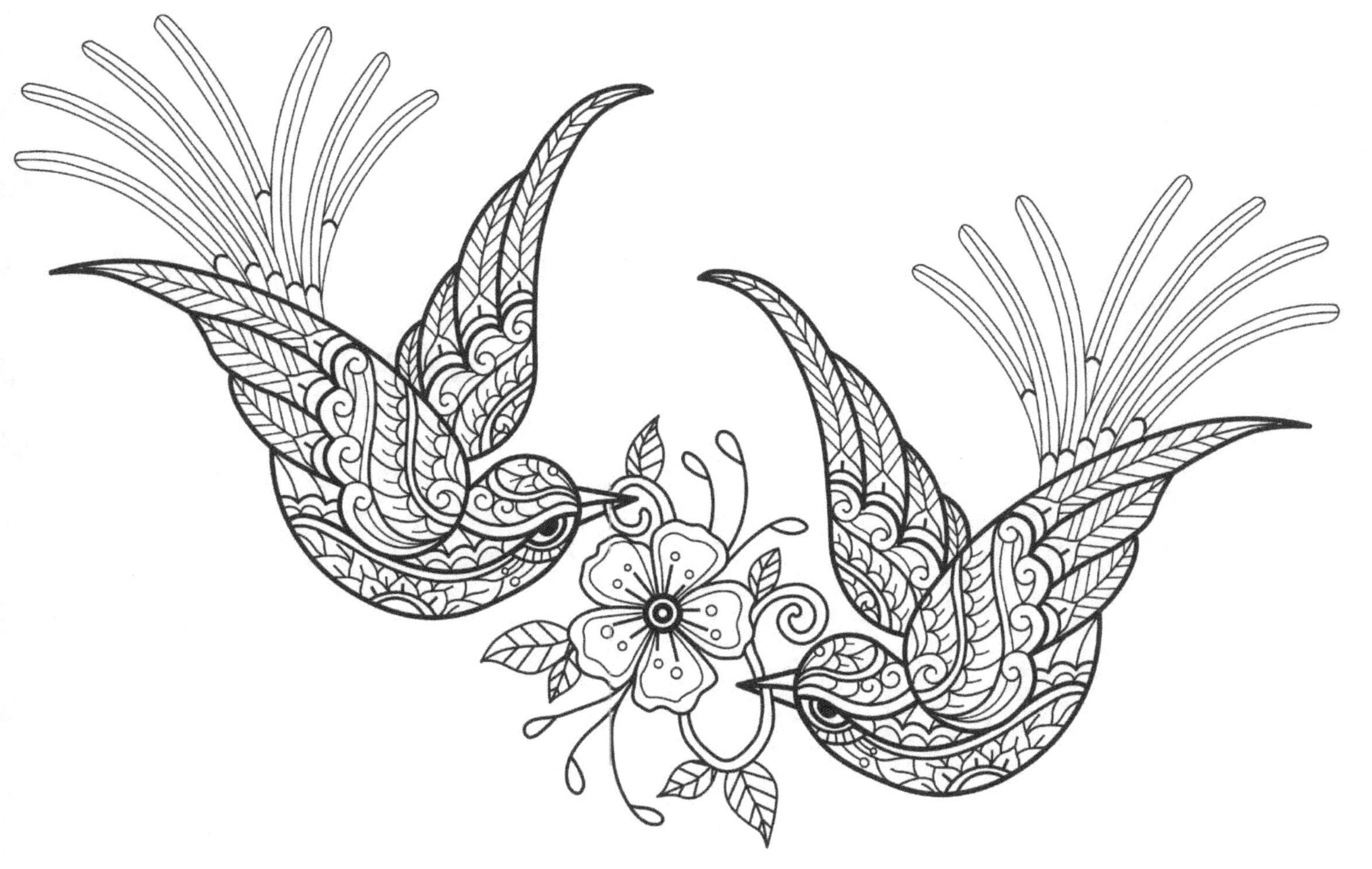

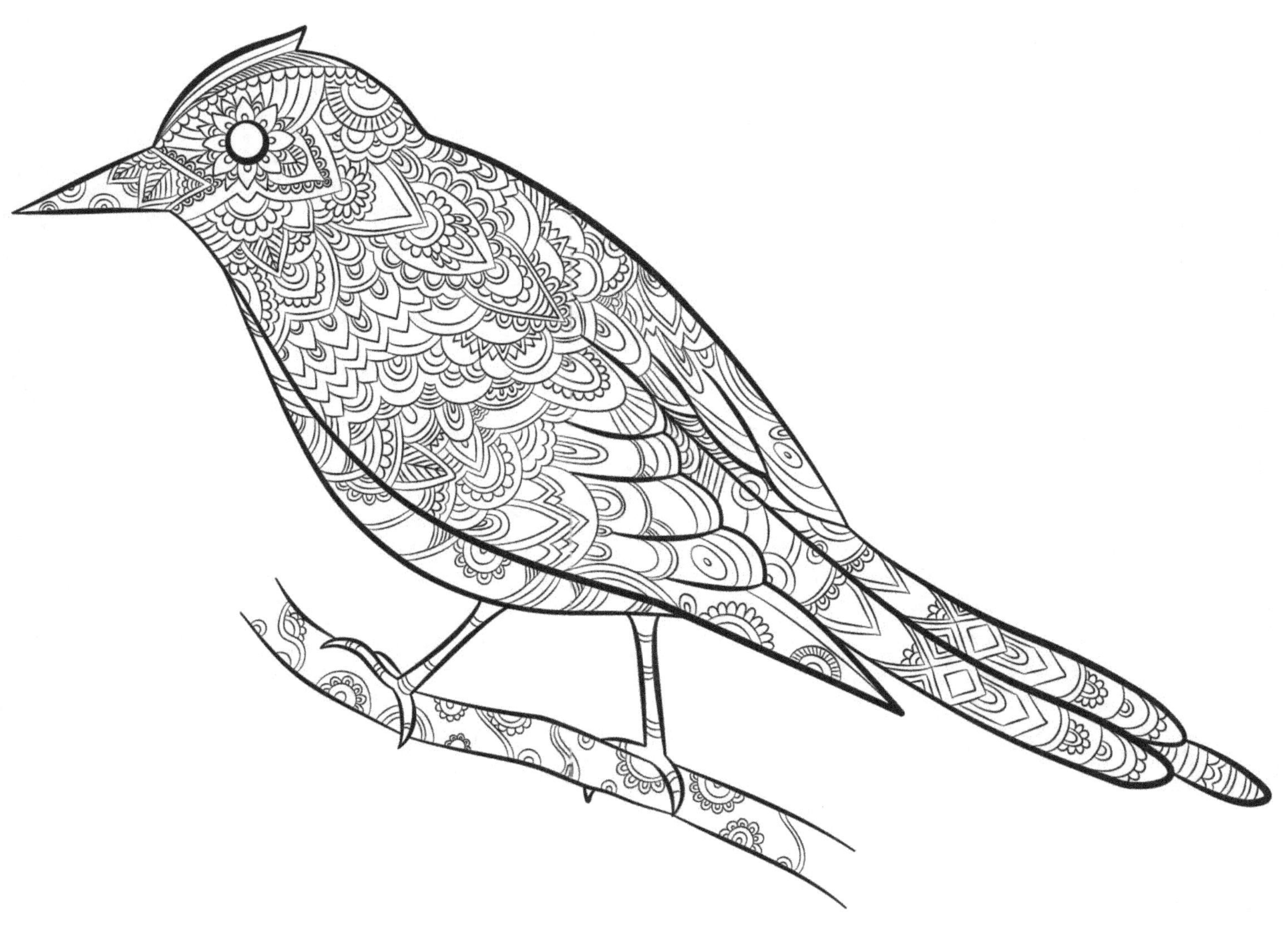

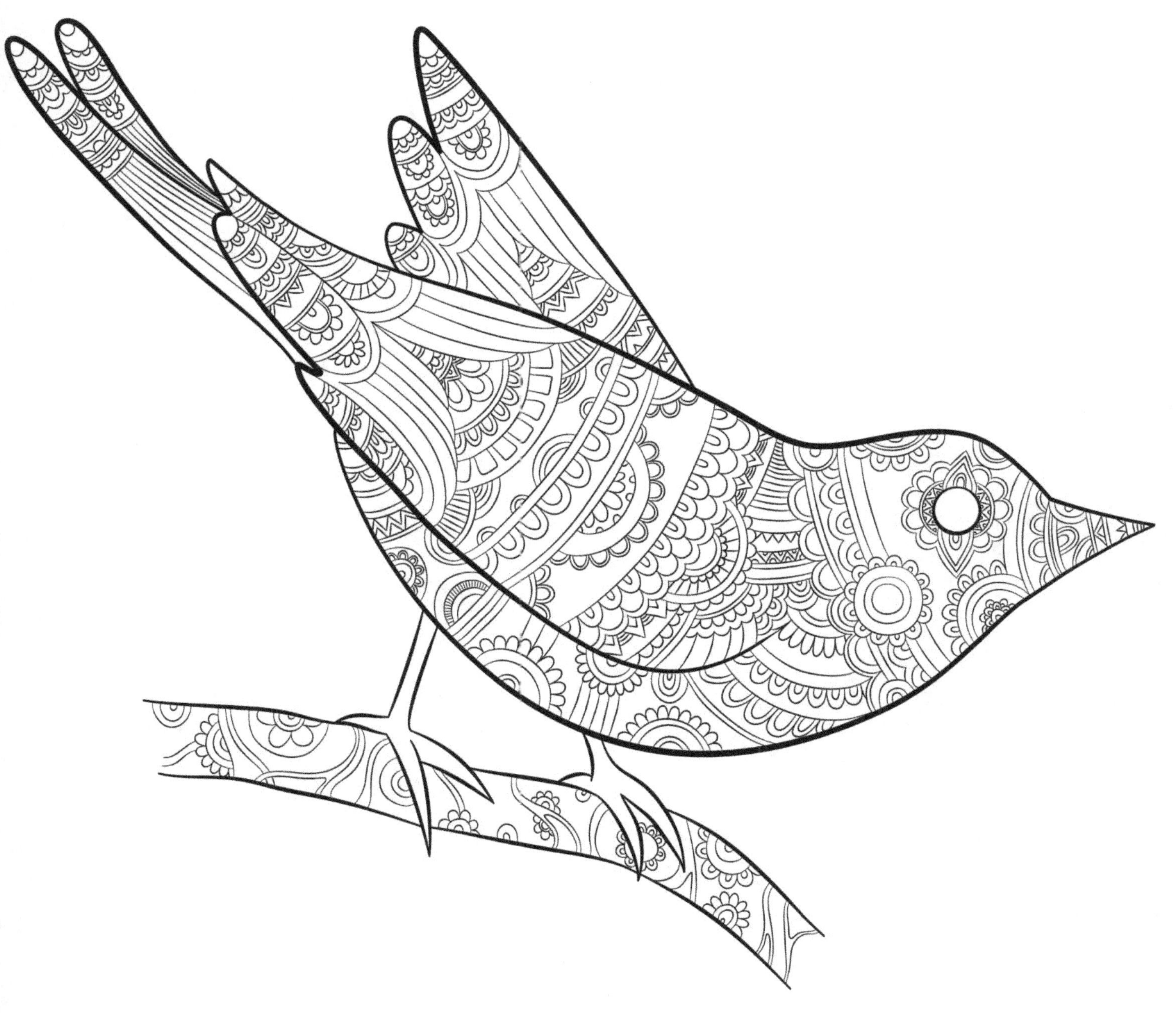

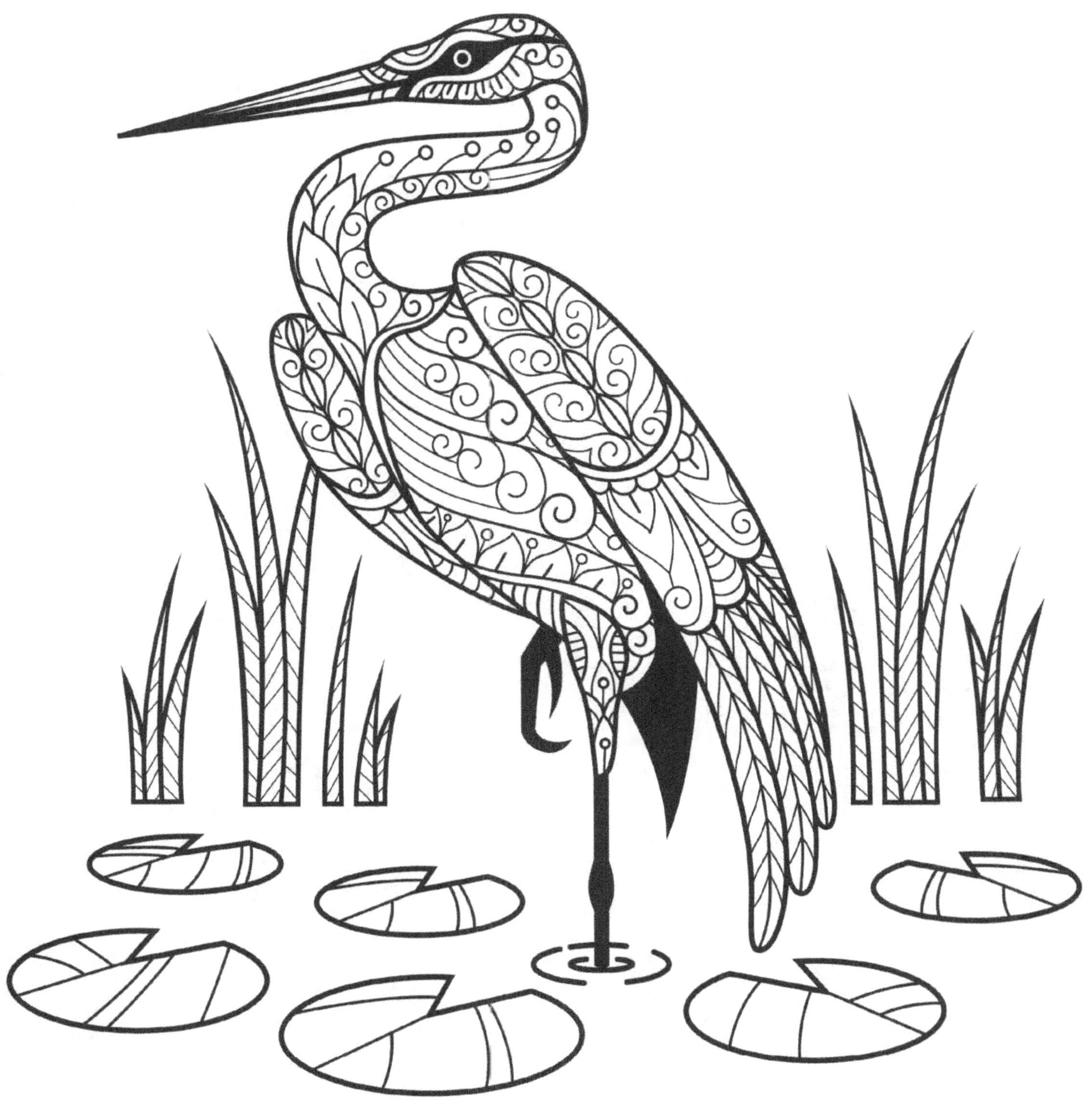

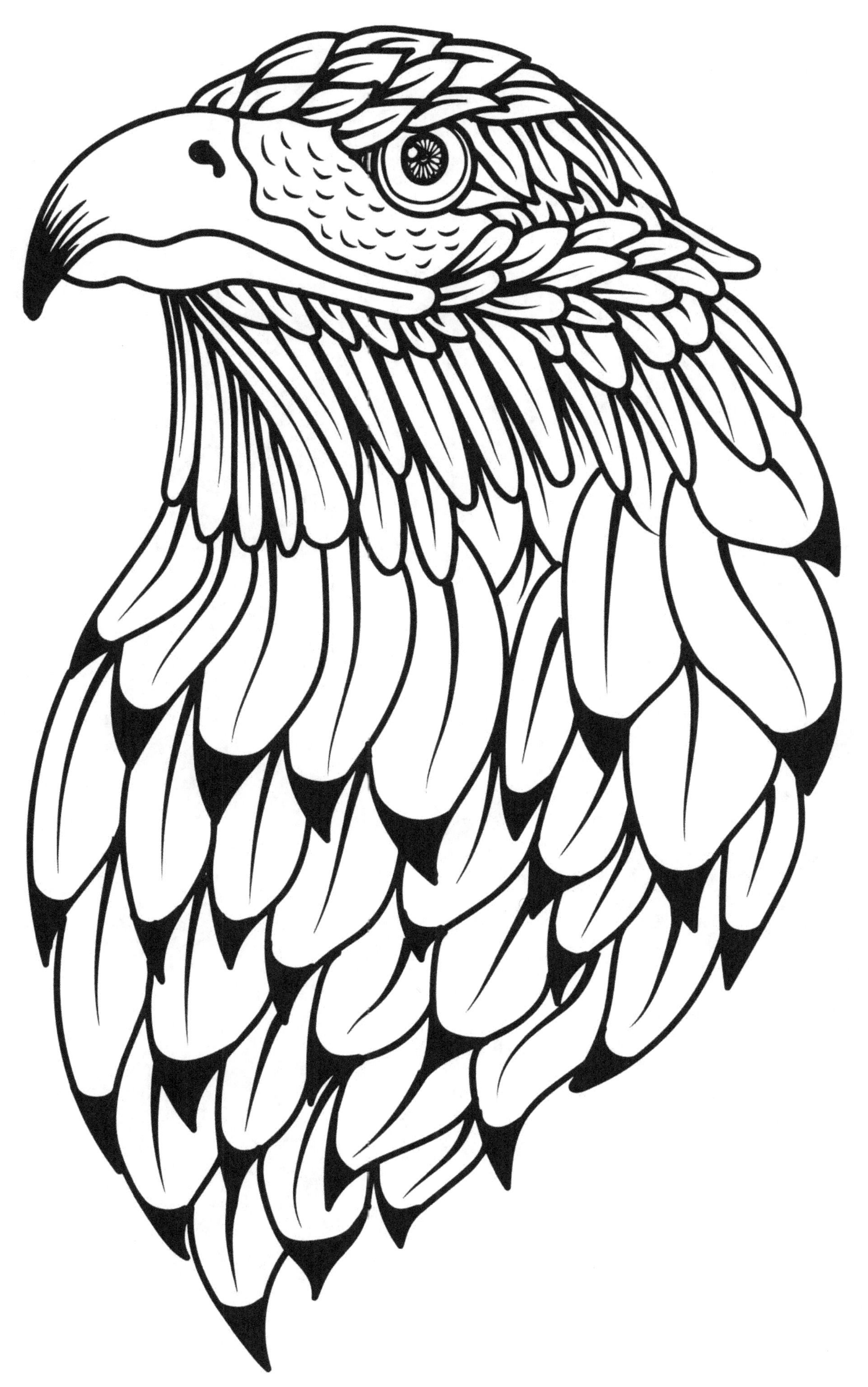

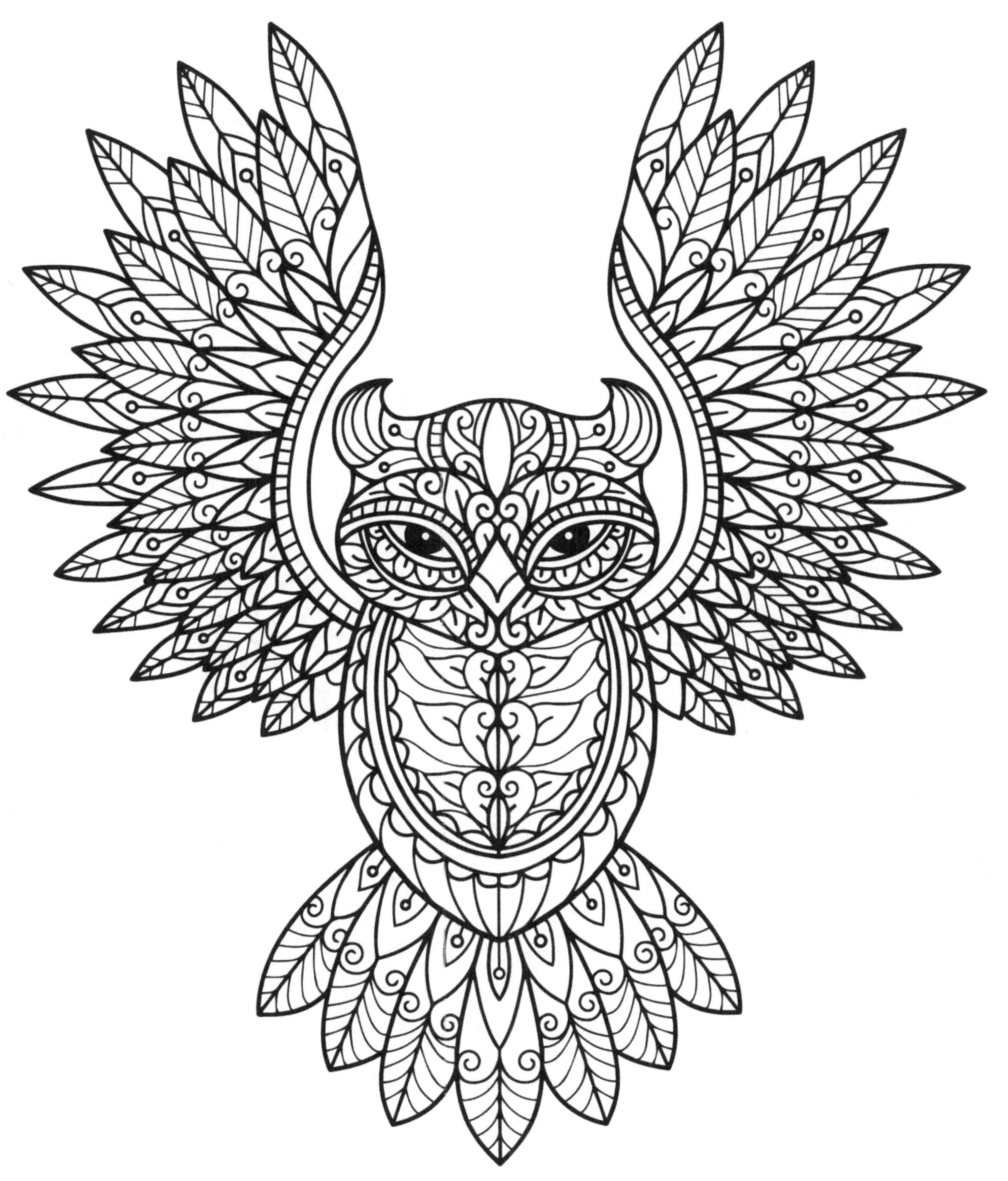

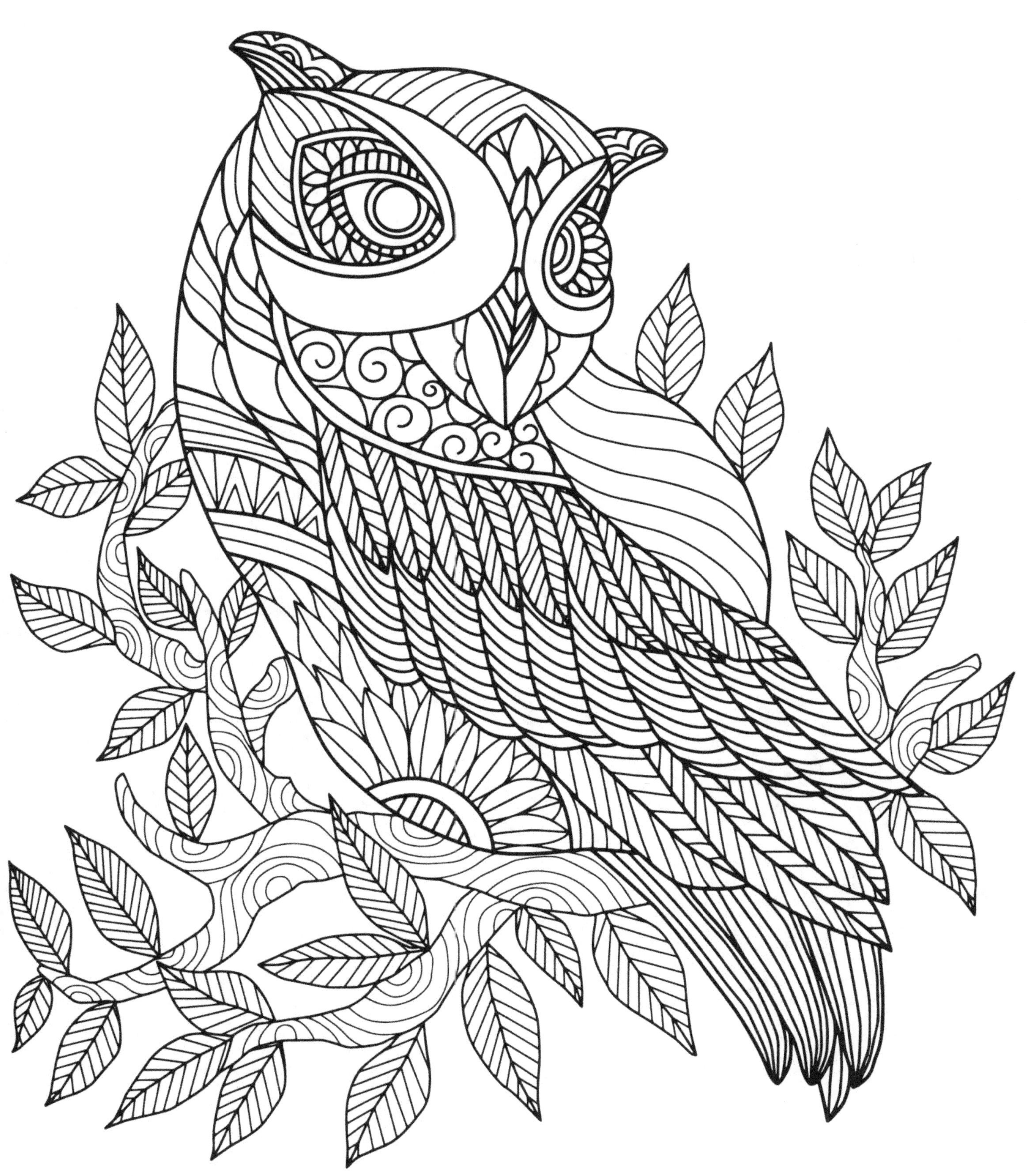

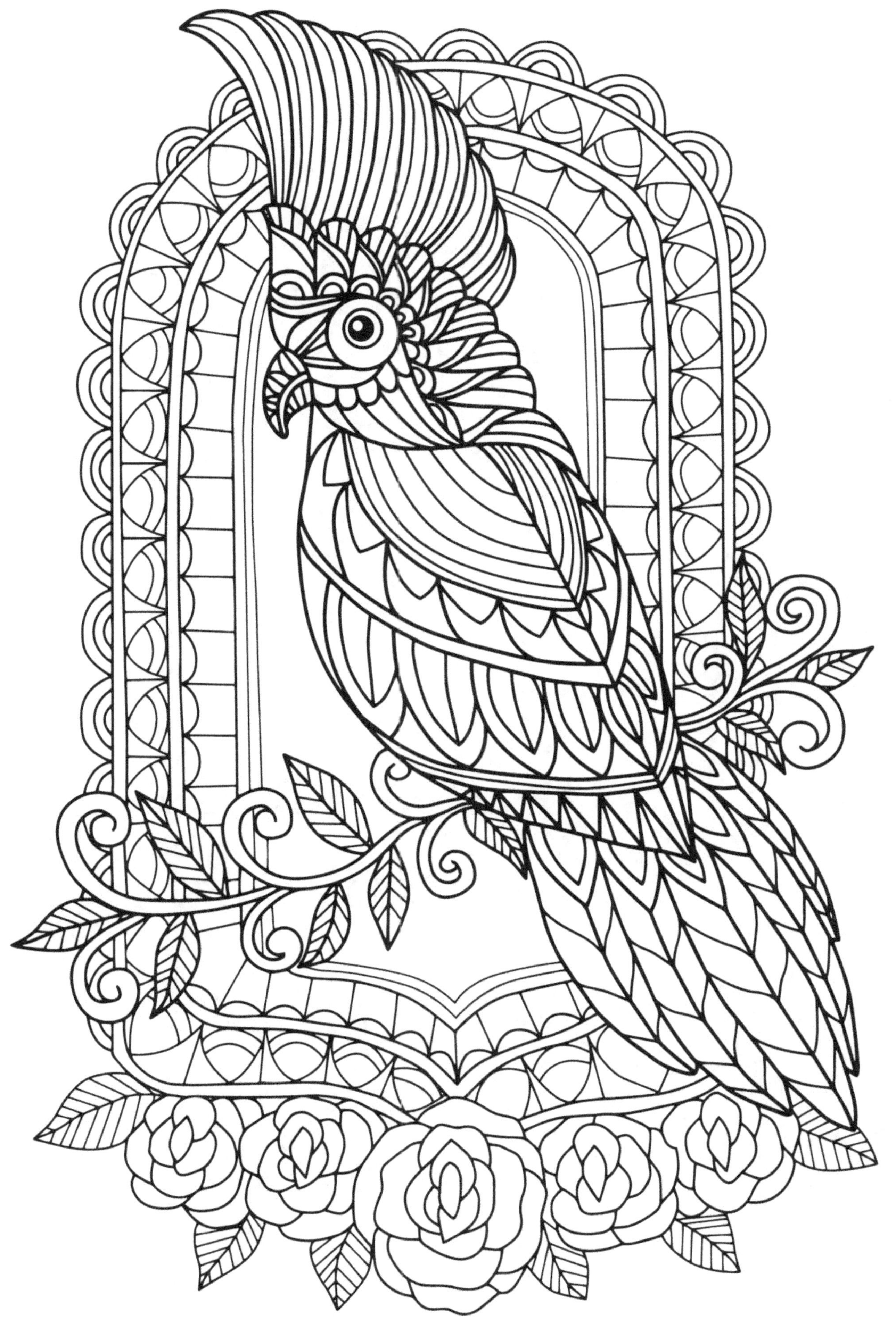

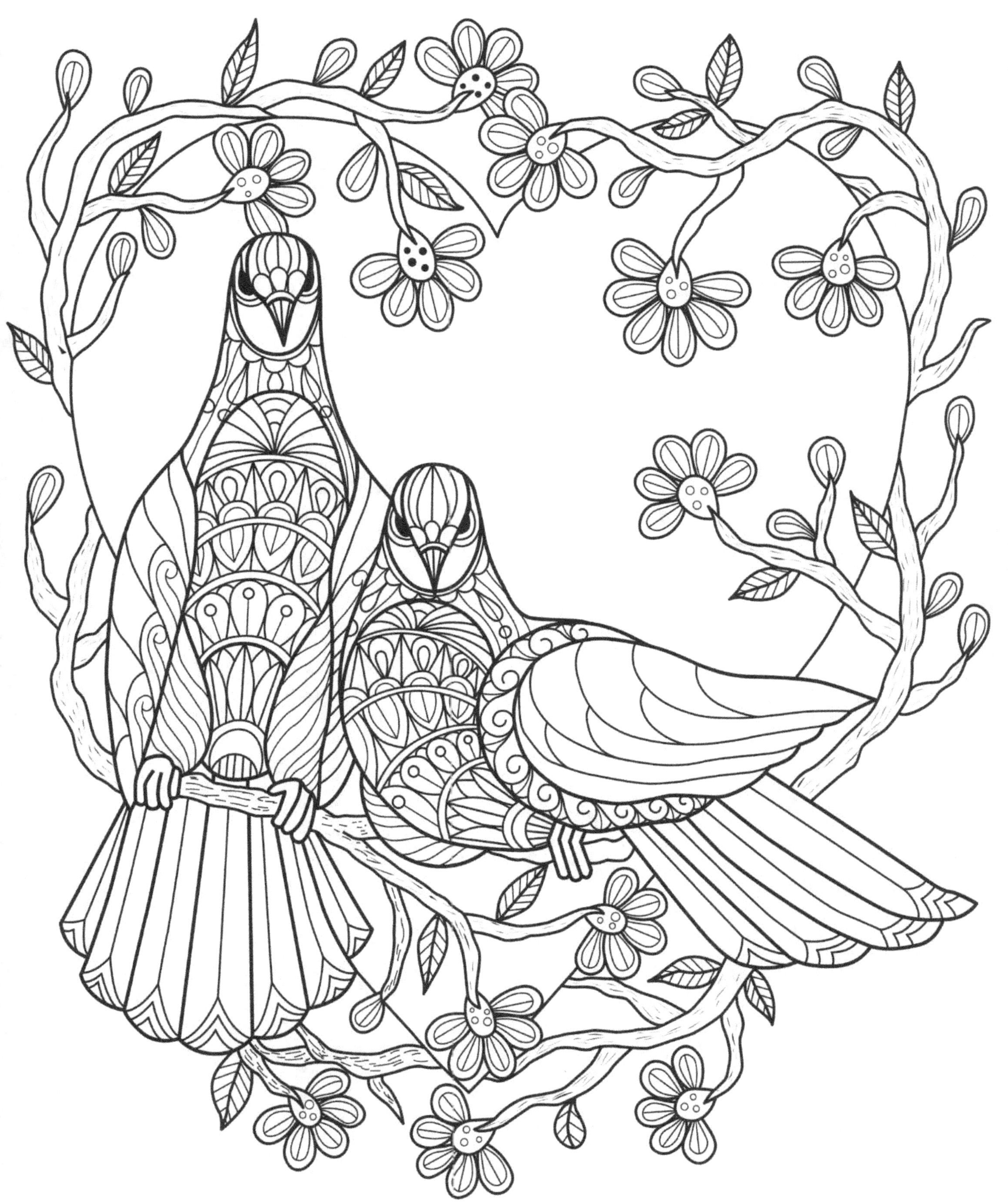

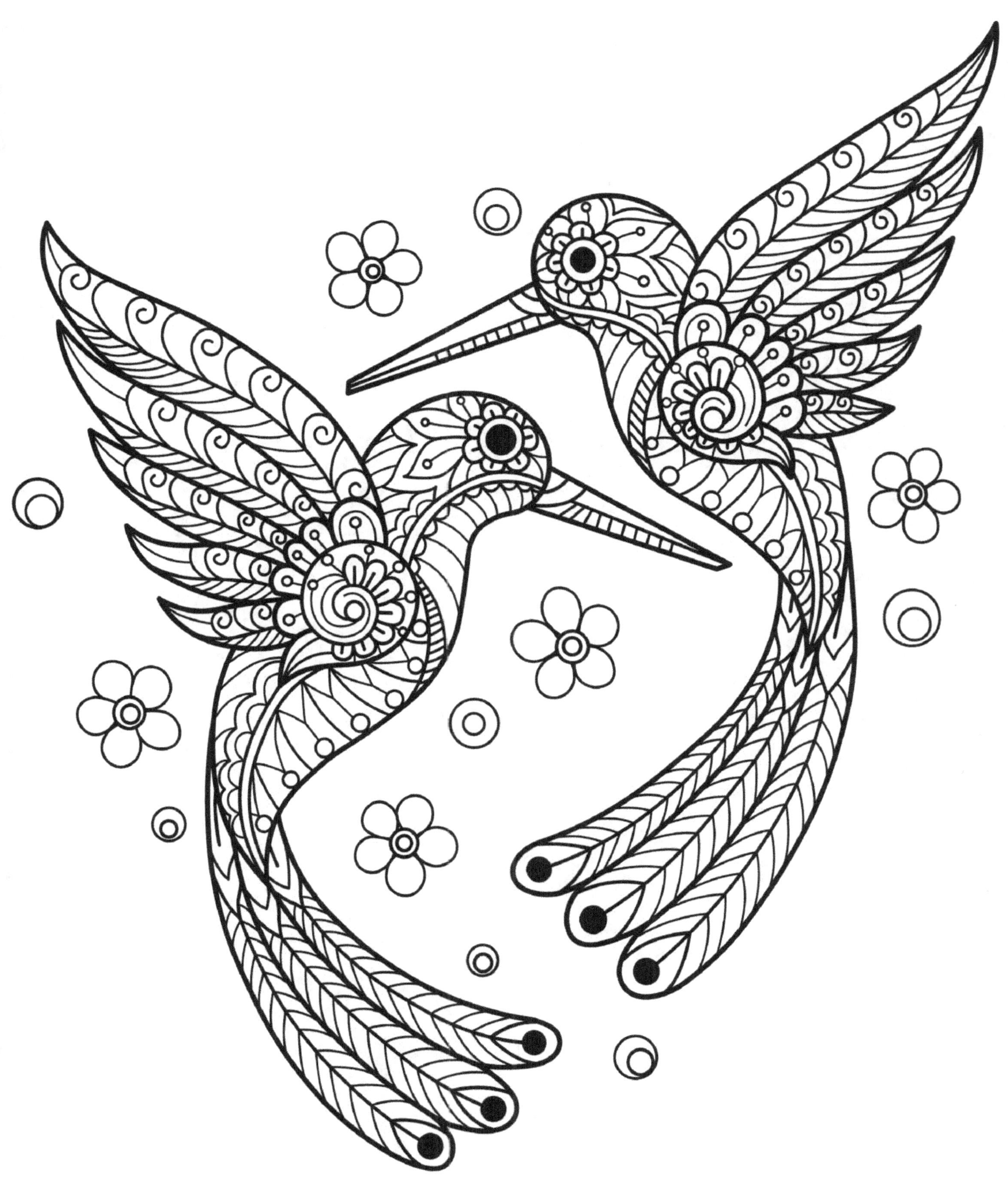

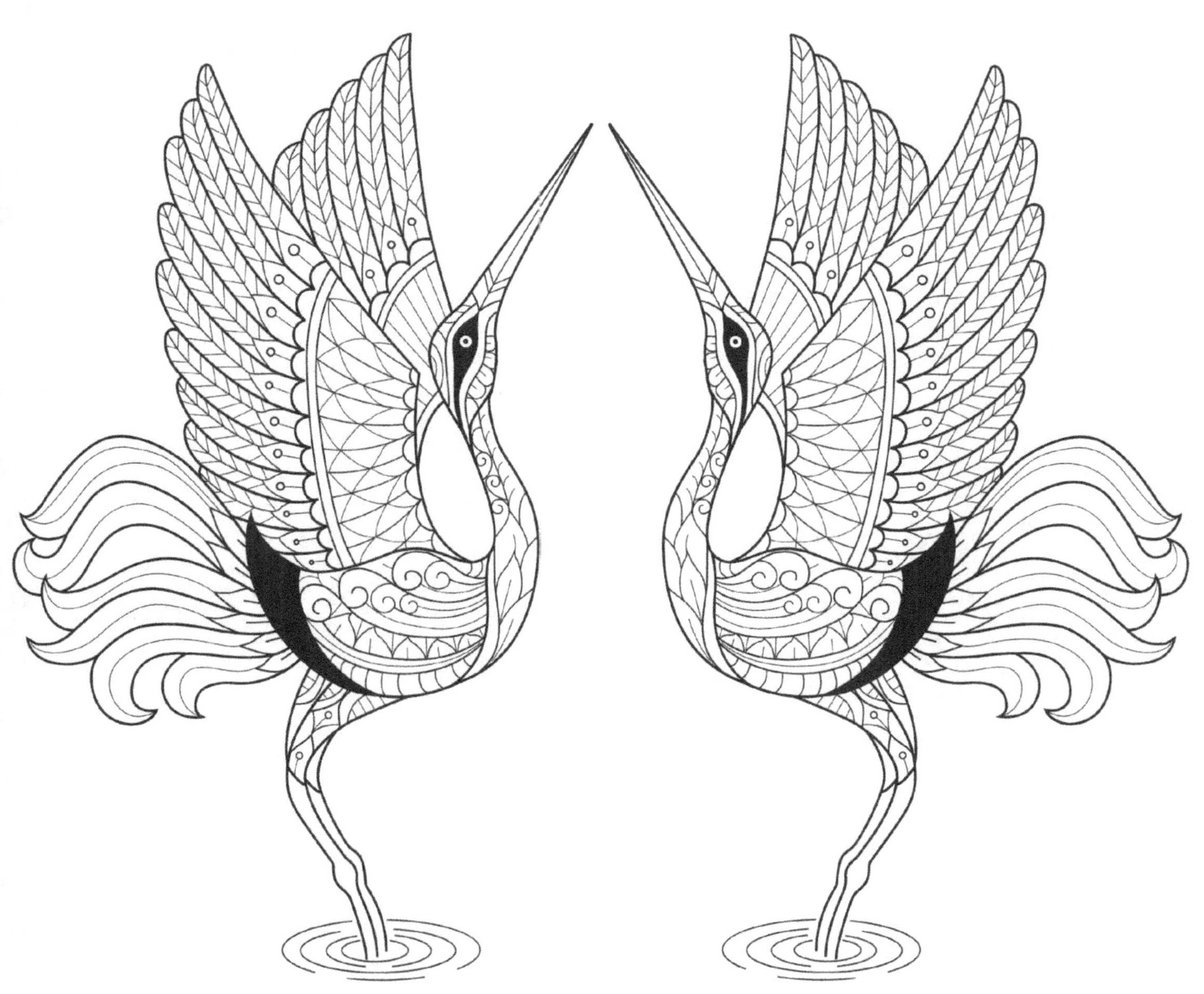

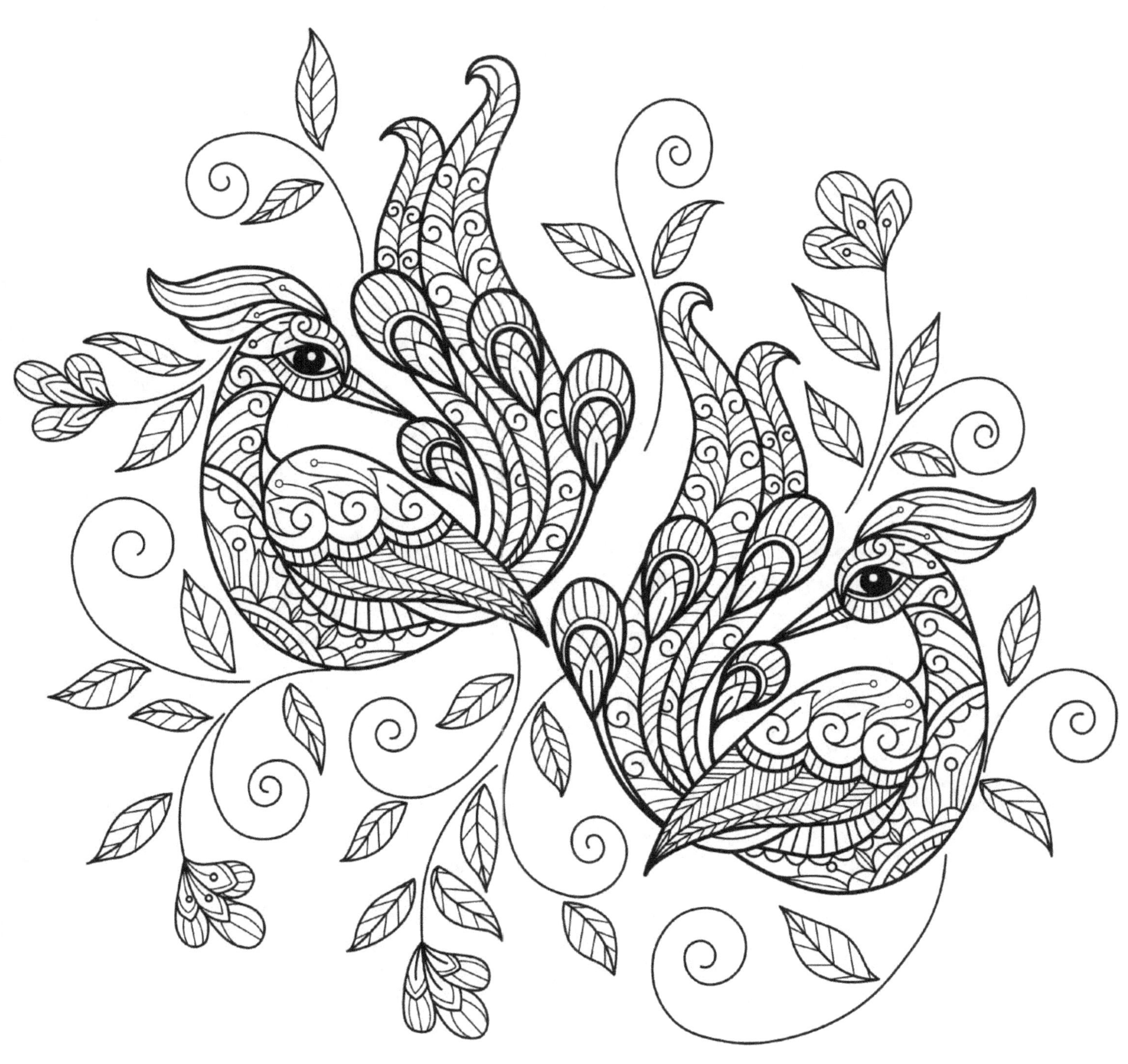

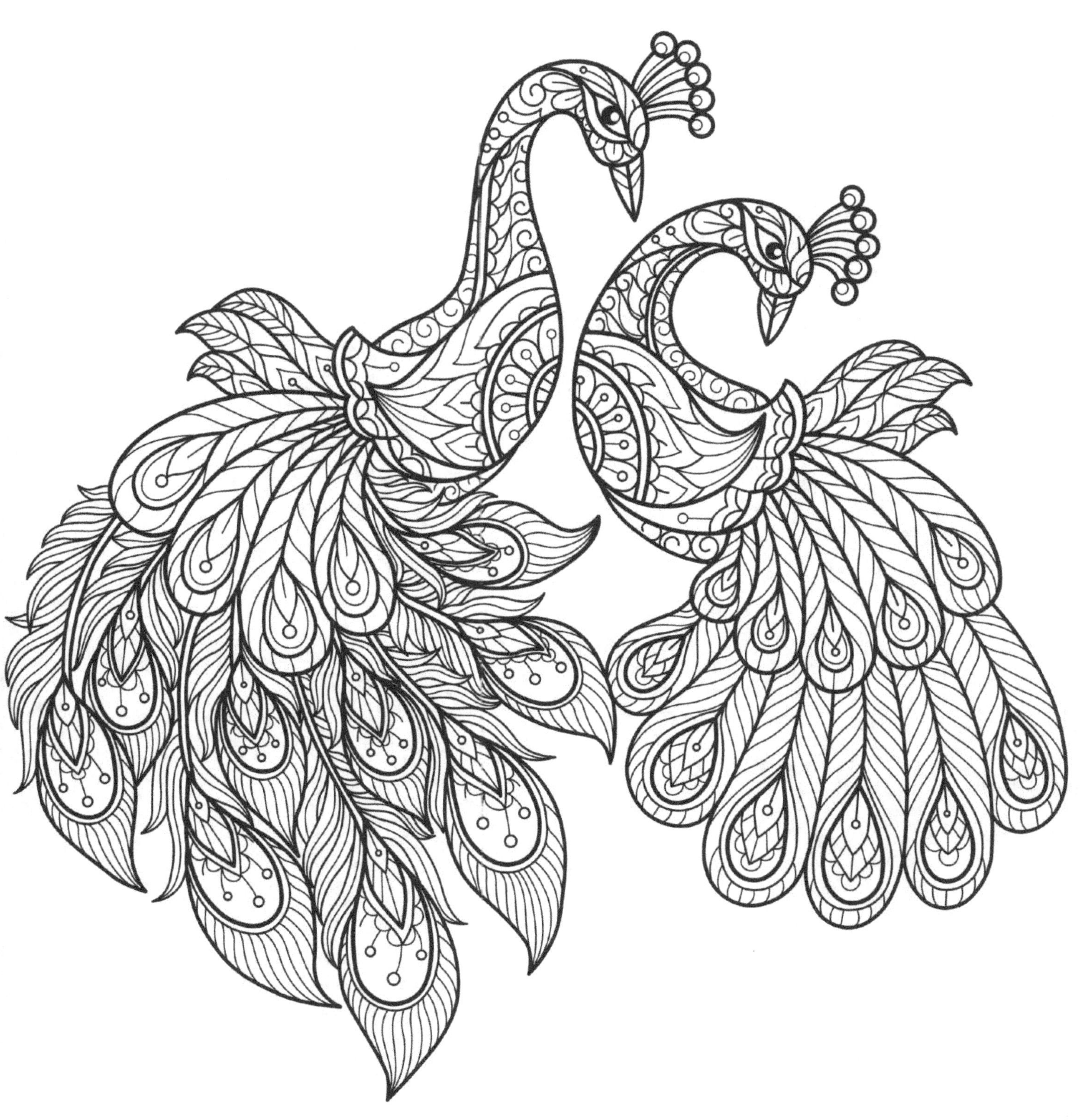

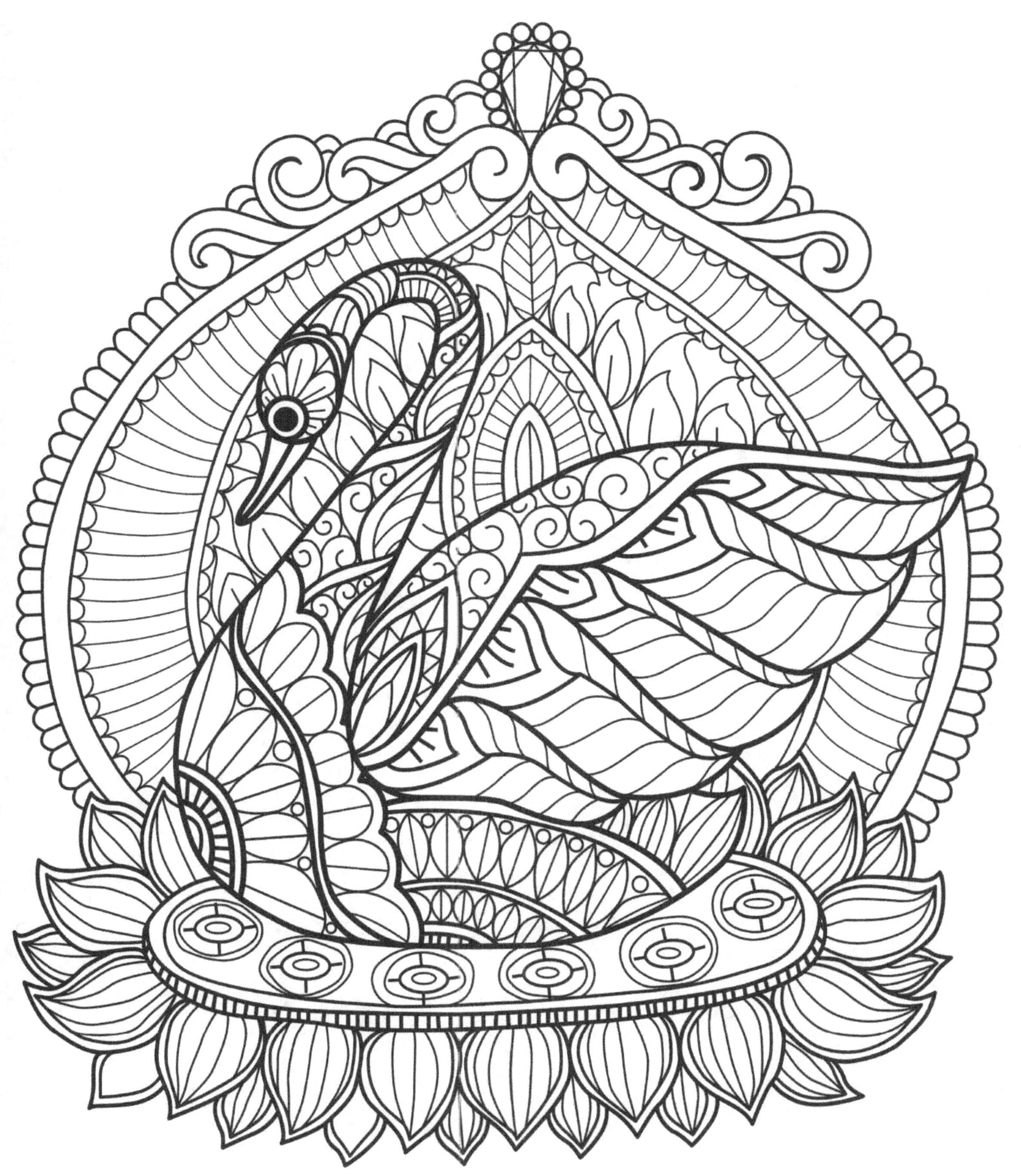

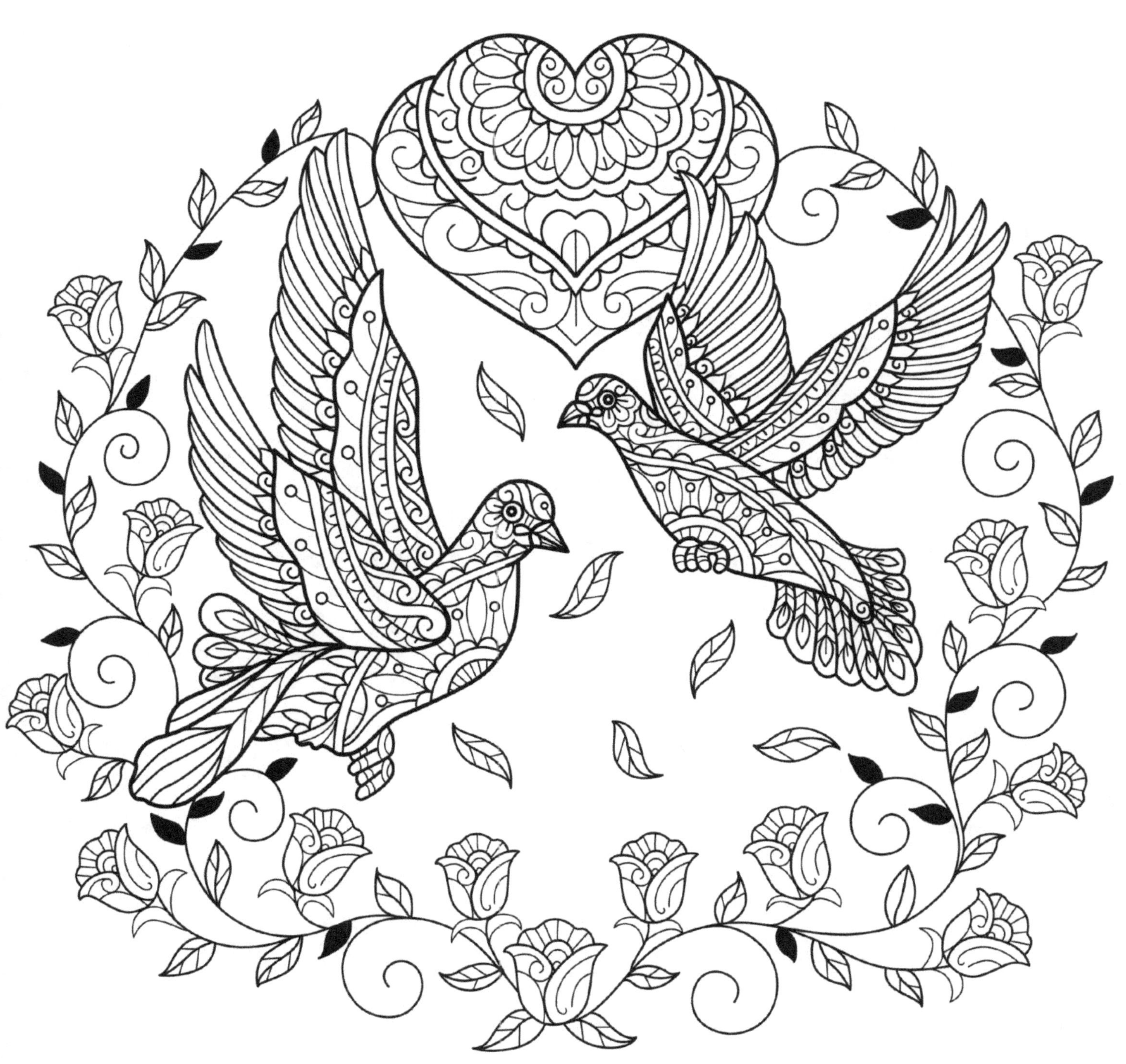

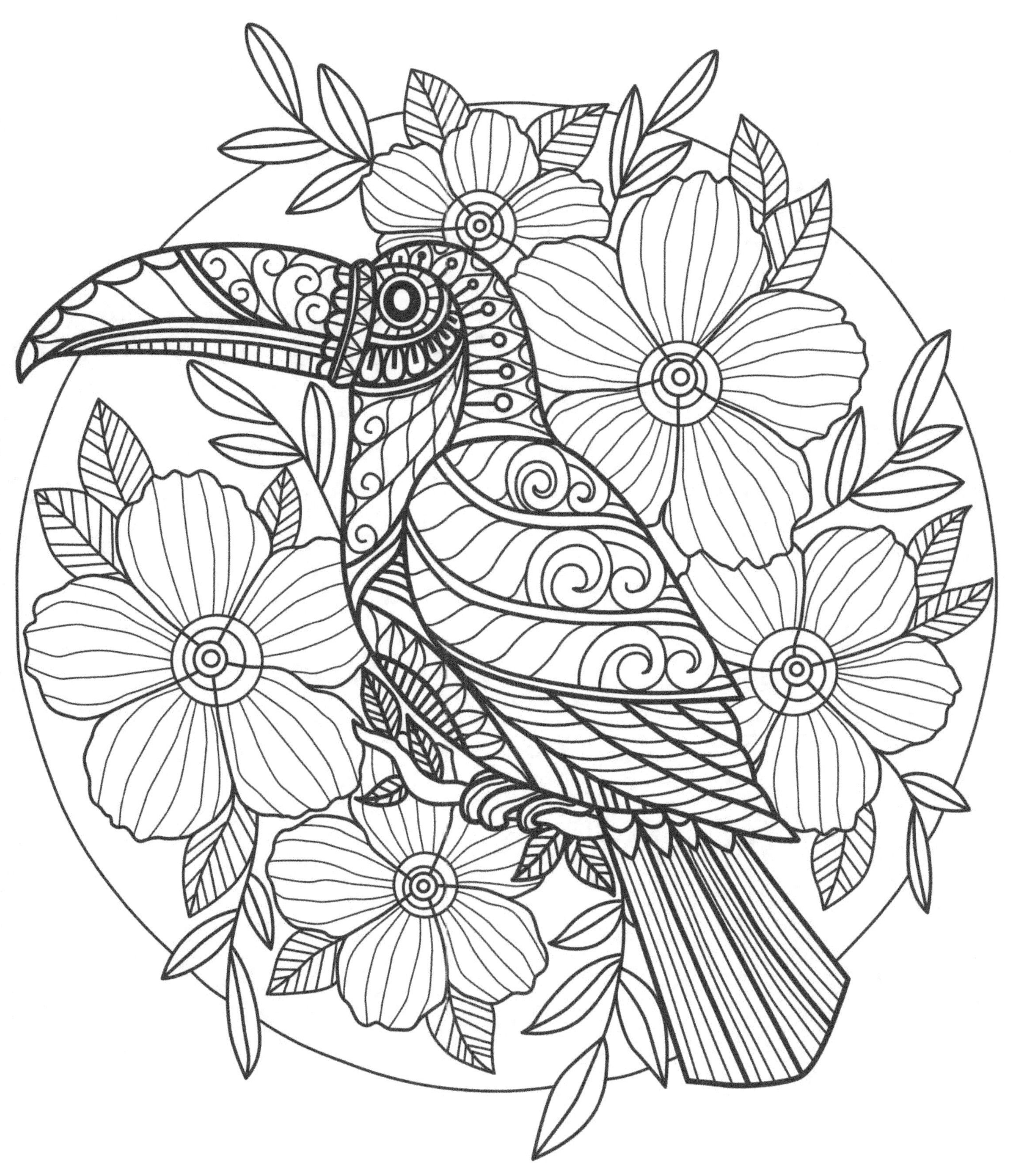

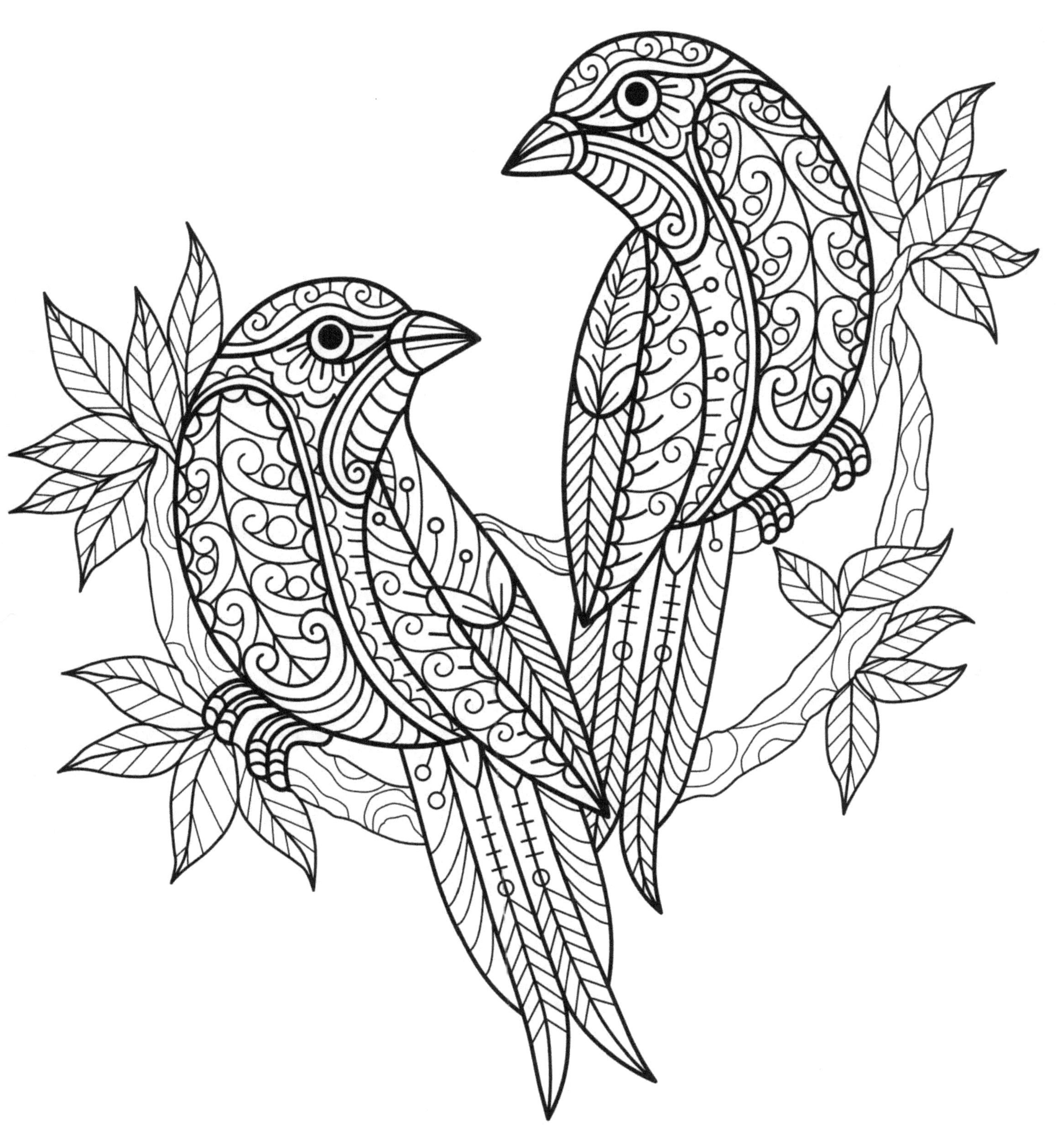

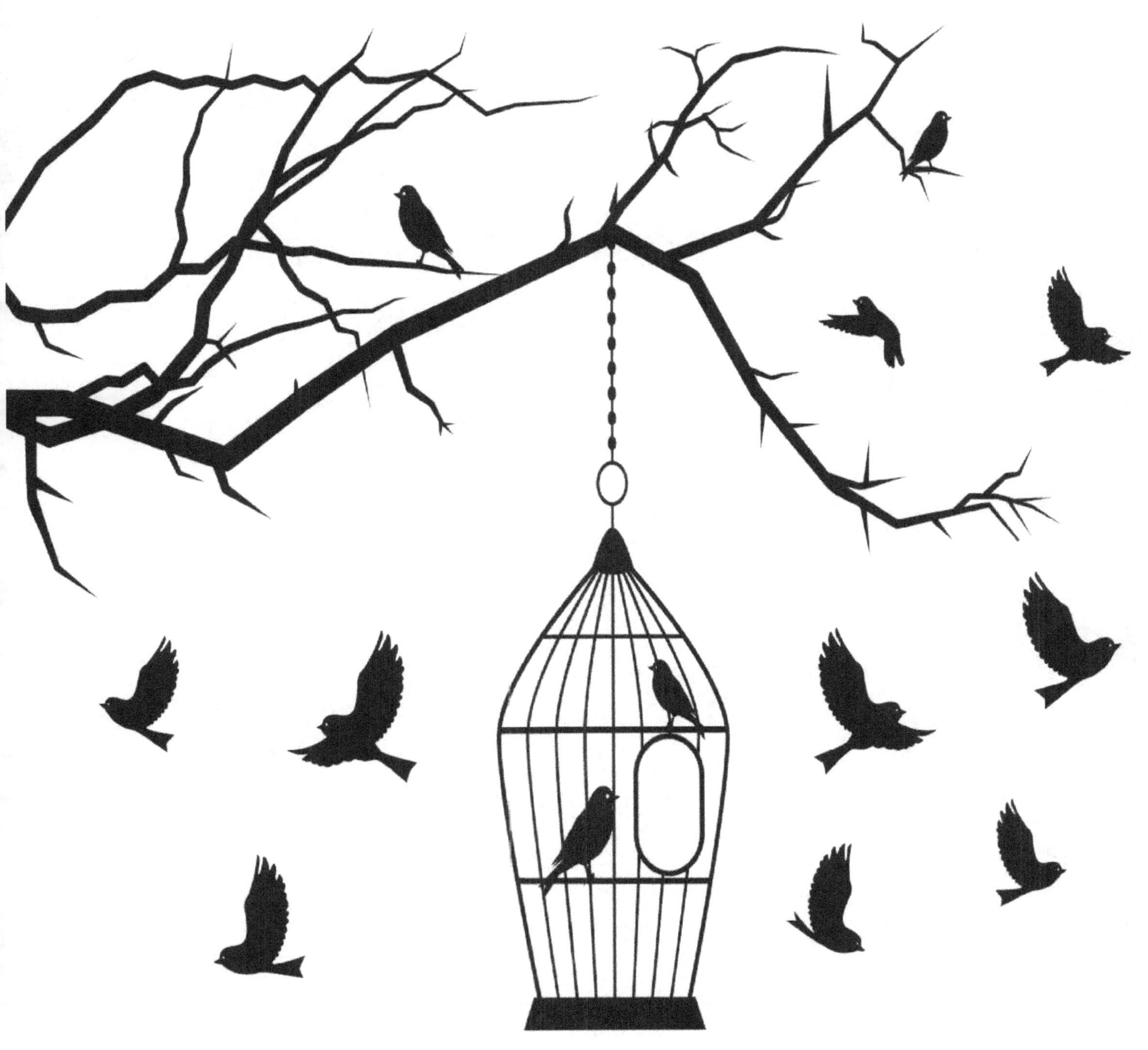